OUR HOME

FROM MAINE ROAD TO THE ETIHAD

100 YEARS

OUR HOME

FROM MAINE ROAD TO THE ETIHAD

100 YEARS

Reach Sport

OUR HOME
FROM MAINE ROAD TO THE ETIHAD
100 YEARS

ISBN: 9781914197857

Writers: Gary James, Kevin Cummins, David Clayton,
Ian Whittell, Simon Monk, Harri Aston
Photography: Victoria Haydn, Tom Flathers, Kevin Cummins
Additional imagery with thanks to Getty Images, PA Images, Colorsport and Mirropix
Production Editor: Simon Monk. Design: Colin Harrison and Lee Ashun
Cover Design: Manchester City FC

First published in Great Britain and Ireland in 2023
by Reach Sport, a part of Reach PLC Ltd

Reach Sport

www.reachsport.com

Printed by Bell & Bain

MIX
Paper | Supporting
responsible forestry
FSC® C007785

CONTENTS

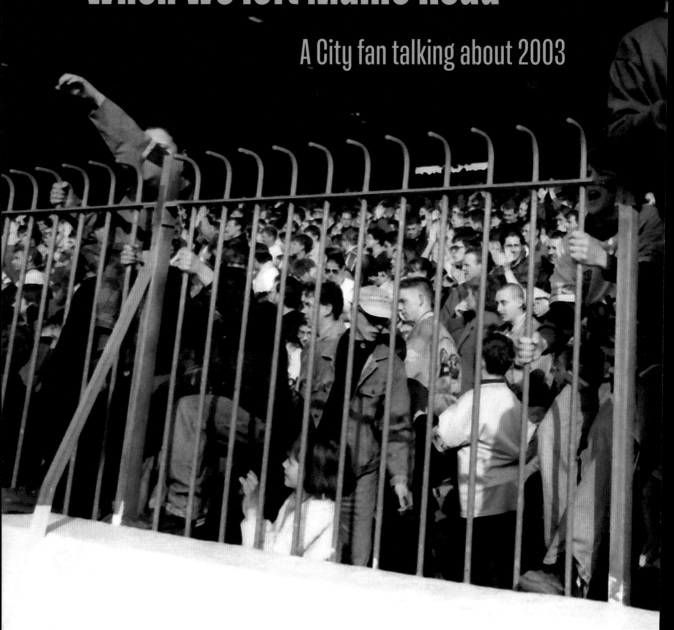

'You couldn't beat the Kippax for energy and passion. Great memories, great times. I cried when we left Maine Road'

A City fan talking about 2003

'Here in this stadium we are something special this season'

Pep Guardiola, Treble-winning manager, 2023

MY HOME

By Mike Summerbee

It's quite fitting that the 100-year anniversary of Maine Road and the 20-year anniversary of the Etihad Stadium should fall on the back of Manchester City's greatest-ever season.

This wonderful football club has been winning trophies for close on 120 years, filling our home stadiums with record numbers and as Club Ambassador, I can't tell you how privileged I feel to be in the position I am in.

My association with City began in 1965 when I signed from Swindon Town at what was the beginning of the Joe Mercer and Malcolm Allison era.

Our goal was to win matches, but to do so with style – not to mention a touch of steel and swagger.

Maine Road was our perfect platform to do just that, with a packed Kippax down one side of the pitch giving us a huge advantage in the games that mattered most because the noise was constant rather than if we just attacked one end.

We had a wonderful playing surface thanks to groundsman Stan Gibson and Maine Road was always a big, expansive pitch that suited our playing style.

Of course, City moved to Maine Road in 1924, long before I was born and used to house enormous crowds – one being 84,569 against Stoke in 1934 which is still a record for an English domestic crowd outside of Wembley.

Fantastic footballers like Peter Doherty, Sam Cowan, Roy Paul and Bert Trautmann graced Maine Road in the years before I came and Francis Lee, Neil Young, Colin Bell and many others in the years after.

During my time, we won plenty of trophies there and some many wonderful memories were created – the 'Ballet on Ice' will always stick in my mind.

Of course, the time was right to relocate to the City of Manchester Stadium in 2003 and like any move to a new home, it takes time to settle in.

But the memories we have created in what is now the Etihad Stadium have made this a genuine home from home.

In fact, in 2022/23 – our Treble-winning season under the wonderful leadership of our most successful manager, Pep Guardiola – the Etihad felt more like a fortress than ever, with the noise and colour making every game an occasion to be relished.

Maine Road was our home for 80 years and will never be forgotten, but the Etihad Stadium has been the setting of some truly unforgettable moments – too many to mention, in fact – and all created playing beautiful football, while our fans created a fantastic atmosphere.

There are many more chapters to be written at the Etihad Stadium, but this book looks back lovingly at 100 years of the places we called – and call – home.

Great players, great managers, and great moments. I hope it brings back as many happy memories for you as it has for me.

Mike Summerbee OBE, June 2023

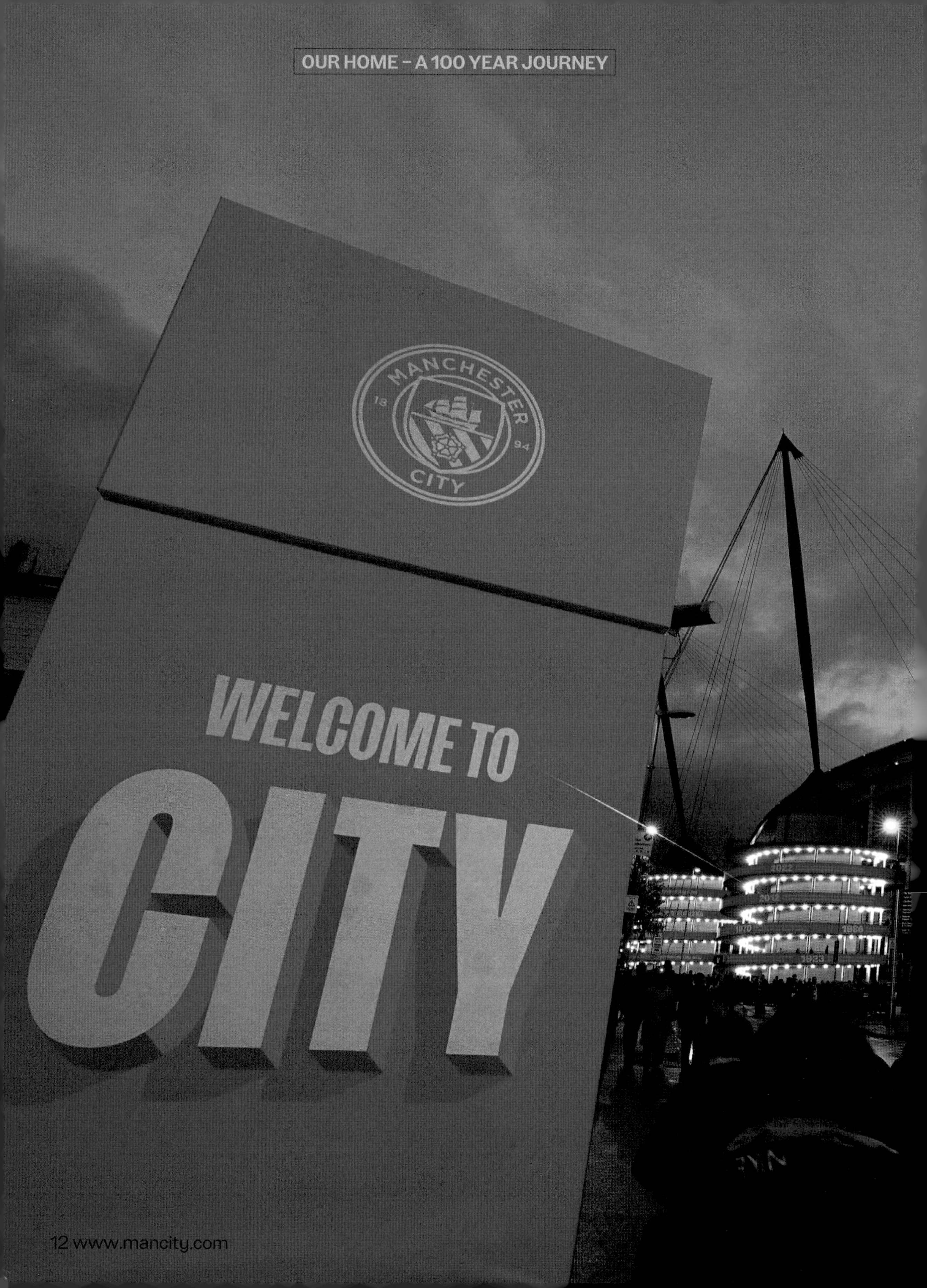
MANCHESTER
18
94
CITY
WELCOME TO
CITY

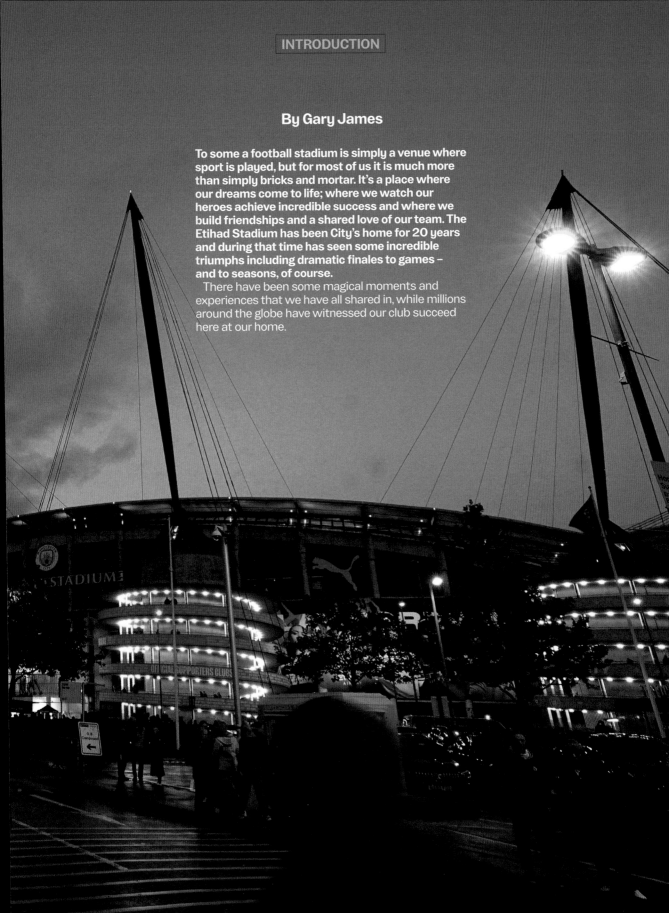

By Gary James

To some a football stadium is simply a venue where sport is played, but for most of us it is much more than simply bricks and mortar. It's a place where our dreams come to life; where we watch our heroes achieve incredible success and where we build friendships and a shared love of our team. The Etihad Stadium has been City's home for 20 years and during that time has seen some incredible triumphs including dramatic finales to games – and to seasons, of course.

There have been some magical moments and experiences that we have all shared in, while millions around the globe have witnessed our club succeed here at our home.

City take on Bolton in the 1904 FA Cup final in London, with Billy Meredith in the thick of the action

The Etihad has also grown and developed. Originally built for the 2002 Commonwealth Games, it was always planned that the stadium would be developed to become a major footballing venue, but our success over the last decade has meant that our home has had to grow further than originally anticipated. The increased capacity and investment in facilities has helped ensure that Manchester City remain at the forefront of European football, while further stadium developments are set to occur over the coming years.

The Etihad has been a wonderful home throughout the last two decades but it promises to be even better over the coming years. What a time to be a Blue!

Of course, City's story did not start with the Etihad. The club's roots go back around 150 years to the West Gorton area of the city, roughly a mile or so from our current home. In 1880 the earliest known match occurred at Farmer's Field, an area of land off present day Wenlock Way, near St Mark's Church. This was nothing more than a rough piece of land but it was the starting point for an incredible

journey that saw our club develop from a church-based community team into a major power within 25 years.

After the initial season the club played at a variety of homes in the wider Gorton area before establishing its first truly enclosed permanent home at Ardwick in 1887. Known as the Hyde Road ground, this venue off Bennett Street was not too far from St Mark's Church and it became the club's first recognisable stadium. As we're focusing on the club's grounds in this book it's not possible to go into all the activities of those formative years. Suffice to say that when the newly named Manchester City were established in 1894, Hyde Road remained home to our club.

Hyde Road grew with the club and in only Manchester City's second season the club were already the league's third best supported side behind Everton and Aston Villa. An amazing feat when you consider that City were a second-tier club at this point. Sixteen years later and we topped the attendance chart for the first time with Hyde Road proving to be a passionate home, even if it was not the most attractive venue around.

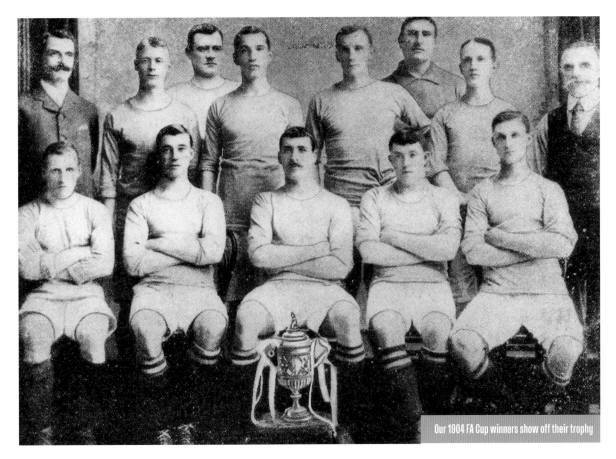

Our 1904 FA Cup winners show off their trophy

Major success came for City in 1904 when we won the FA Cup for the first time. This, incidentally, was the first major trophy won by either Manchester club and it helped establish the Blues as Manchester's team. What also helped cement City as *the* team locally at that time was the ground itself. Hyde Road housed an unusual corner stand known as the Boys Stand. This stand, free from parental influence, became renowned for developing a powerful atmosphere and young fans eagerly waited to graduate to the Boys Stand as they grew.

By 1910 Hyde Road regularly held about 40,000 for games but access to the stadium was difficult and often gates were closed by order of the police some way off capacity. Almost every game was a logistical nightmare and the issue was frequently discussed. *The Book of Football*, published in 1905, commented: "Manchester City get exceptionally big gates, and they would get larger did they possess a better constructed and more commodious ground. That is their chief want."

City did frequently improve the venue and in 1910 the ground had a roof on every side and boasted of covered accommodation for 35,000 people in a 40,000 capacity. A huge number for the time and in contrast to around 10,000 covered places at the recently opened Old Trafford.

During World War One Hyde Road continued to stage games but it was also used for military purposes. Fans were encouraged to participate in military drills, while horses were stabled there for a time.

After the war, demand to watch the Blues continued to increase and Hyde Road's capacity continued to be tested. Then, between March 1920 and March 1921, three major events occurred at City's home.

King George V meets the Manchester City players at Hyde Road in 1920

Firstly, King George V attended a 2-1 victory over Liverpool in March 1920. This was the first time a reigning monarch had attended a game outside of London. Then the following November the club's Main Stand was destroyed in a fire. The Blues hoped to move temporarily to Old Trafford but media reports claimed United's rent demands were too high, so City soldiered on at Hyde Road.

Finally, a crucial game with Burnley in March 1921 was watched by probably the greatest crowd ever housed at the old ground when an estimated 60,000 people (officially 40,000) poured into the stadium. Gates were smashed down and the need for a bigger venue was clear.

The club had been looking to build a new stadium for decades, but in May 1922 the news broke that City were to move to the border of Rusholme and Moss Side. The idea was that they would build a new 120,000 capacity stadium which they hoped would be regarded as 'The English Hampden'. At this time Hampden Park was recognised as the greatest stadium in the world and linking City's plans to it demonstrated that the new home was not going to be any old stadium – it was aiming to be the best.

The development of Maine Road occurred at the same time as Wembley Stadium was being constructed, and as Sir Robert McAlpine & Sons were the builders of both venues there was a great deal of rivalry between their northern and southern divisions. The Empire Stadium, as it was known at the time, simply had to be finished for the 1923 Cup final, while Maine Road had an anticipated completion date of September 1923.

As many Blues suspected at the time, the original 120,000 capacity plans were a little over the top and by the

City goalkeeper Len Langford at Maine Road in 1933

time the serious development work commenced City had decided that there would be a 10,000 capacity Main Stand, with terracing holding around 75,000 surrounding the rest of the pitch. This was still a phenomenal figure for a team used to playing in a cramped 40,000 capacity venue, and it demonstrated the club's ambition.

The new stadium was to become known as Maine Road, after the street it was built on. The street had originally been called Dog Kennel Lane but was renamed several decades earlier after consultation with the Temperance Movement. The new name commemorated a temperance law passed in the state of Maine during the 1850s.

The stadium opened in 1923 and within a year attracted 76,166 to an FA Cup tie against Cardiff. This was the largest crowd ever assembled at an English club ground and a record

for any game outside of London. The figure was eclipsed a decade later when 84,569 watched City defeat Stoke 1-0 on March 3, 1934 and that attendance remains the highest crowd ever at a club ground and again, the highest English attendance outside of London. This means that via these two attendance records, City will have been the record holder for over a century in 2024.

Like the Etihad, Maine Road was extended and improved several times in its first couple of decades. The Main Stand/Platt Lane corner was rebuilt and roofed to include additional terracing and 950 extra seats in 1931 then, four years later, the rest of the Platt Lane end was roofed and extended. This brought the capacity up to over 85,000.

The 1930s were glorious years for both City and Maine Road with the stadium providing the main backdrop to significant FA Cup ties and then, in 1936/37, the club's first league

Blues keeper Bert Trautmann stops a Manchester United attack at Maine Road in 1955

championship. A 4-1 victory over Sheffield Wednesday in the penultimate league game brought wild celebrations, including a pitch invasion.

When war came in 1939 Maine Road continued to host games but, as with Hyde Road, the stadium was chosen to play its part in the war effort. It housed important supplies which were stored in the tunnels and within the Main Stand. The surrounding streets saw some houses hit during air raids but Maine Road itself survived. Across at Old Trafford the situation was somewhat different and United's ground was hit by bombs. City immediately offered United the use of Maine Road and agreement letters show that the terms were ones that the Reds themselves had suggested.

United stayed at Maine Road until 1949 and they established their own record crowd, which City officials calculated as 83,260. This remains the highest league attendance. City had created another milestone during

this time when 69,463 watched the Blues beat Burnley 1-0 in May 1947. At the time this was a record crowd for a second-tier match.

During the 1950s City found major success and the stadium was improved again. In 1953 floodlights were erected, which led to United once again being offered the use of City's stadium. United were hoping to participate in the 1956/57 European Cup but Old Trafford did not possess floodlights and so City offered to stage the games. Many Blues attended these showpiece European games and 75,598 watched one match.

Further stadium improvements came in 1957 when the terracing opposite the Main Stand was extended a little and roofed. Originally known as the Popular Side, the decision was taken to rename the terracing and the Kippax Street Stand was born. Prior to 1957 the noisier fans tended to stand on the Scoreboard End (later North Stand) but over time they drifted into the Kippax. The stand became the singing heartbeat

Rodney Marsh celebrates as City beat United 3-0 at Maine Road in November 1972

of the club from the 1960s through to its demolition in 1994 and fans boasted that while some clubs had 'ends', City's vocal support had an entire 'side'.

The best Maine Road era for many fans was the 1960s and 1970s. The club won the League, FA Cup, League Cup (twice) and the club's first European trophy, the Cup Winners' Cup. During those two decades the ground saw bench seating placed in the Platt Lane; a new Main Stand roof section providing better views for the majority in the stand; taller floodlights and then between 1970 and 1972 a new North Stand was constructed.

This initially held 22,000 standing in 1971 but was adapted a year later to be a seated stand holding 8,120 on grey plastic seats. There had also been major building developments such as the social club, souvenir shop, ticket office and other club facilities. Plans for an enlarged Kippax Stand were discussed but once Peter Swales became chairman in 1973, investment in major developments ended for almost two decades.

There were changes to Maine Road but most of these were connected with safety, security or hospitality such as the development of segregation and perimeter fencing or the conversion of space within the Main Stand for the Executive Suite. Then in 1981/82 the club announced a major redevelopment of the ground. The plans included rebuilding the Platt Lane Stand, re-roofing both the Main and Kippax Stands and installing executive boxes hung from the new Main Stand roof.

City were a very well-supported club by this time and the perception was of a wealthy, powerful major club playing in a major venue. However, a shock relegation highlighted serious financial issues and these meant that only the Main Stand roof was built. Even that was not as planned.

Despite staging many internationals and semi-finals over the years, plus the 1984 League Cup final replay, the

The Commonwealth Games closing ceremony at the City of Manchester Stadium in 2002

stadium was falling behind due to lack of investment. Capacity was reduced following the 1985 Bradford fire and the 1989 Hillsborough disaster and there were serious concerns with the Platt Lane Stand, which included wooden benches and was extended on wooden terracing at the back. All-seater legislation was also coming in and so the club were forced into rebuilding two stands.

First the Platt Lane was replaced with a much smaller capacity new stand, which opened in March 1993, then the Kippax was replaced with a three-tier stand, completed in 1995. These developments meant the permanent capacity of the stadium was only 31,458, the lowest for a City venue since 1904. This was far too low and, despite the club dropping to the third tier for the first time in 1998, additional temporary seating was needed to boost capacity.

One temporary uncovered area became known as the Gene Kelly Stand, because fans sat there 'singing in the rain'. By 2002 additional temporary stands brought the capacity up to 35,150 but it was still not enough.

Alongside these developments, in the 1990s Manchester was bidding to stage the Olympic Games. City had supported the idea from its inception in the 1980s and the club had talked about moving to any venue erected. Initial proposals came in the 1980s for a new stadium where the Trafford Centre was eventually built, but by the time of Manchester's second bid, the plans had been altered with the present-day Etihad Stadium site becoming the final option.

Ultimately, Manchester was not awarded the Olympics but did stage the Commonwealth Games in 2002. Unlike the London Olympic Stadium, Manchester's plan was always to convert the stadium to become a footballing home after the Games. City signed the agreement in 1999 to move to the new ground and it was the club's support of the idea that ensured a permanent stadium could be erected.

The Etihad Stadium in all its glory in 2023

The ground, known as the City of Manchester Stadium at the time, was built in two stages. The first saw what is now the second tier and the two side-stand third tiers built. The athletics track extended out where the North Stand is today and a large temporary stand was built beyond the track at that end.

After the Games the lowest level was dug out and our current first tier was then terraced and seated. The North Stand was erected and when completed the stadium capacity was 47,726 (excluding segregation needs). City personalised the stadium and lounges, such as the Legends Lounge and 1894 Suite, were fitted out. A vote to rename the West Stand saw fans choose to name the stand after Colin Bell.

Over the following few years seats in the stadium were reconfigured at times causing fluctuations in the capacity, however the first major development occurred in 2010 when improvements were made to hospitality areas, the pitch was redeveloped and additional rows of seating were installed pitch-side.

A new third tier was added to the South Stand in 2015 with small extensions to the southern ends of the Colin Bell and East Stands' third tiers. Further seating changes have been made since then, and the next few years will see major developments at the North Stand and a further increase in capacity and facilities due to demand.

Since 2011 major success has returned to City while the Etihad, as it is now known, has become a wonderful and worthy home for a successful club with ambition.

Since joining the league the Blues have been based at three major venues. Each one has enjoyed representative international games; major neutral matches; women's football; royal visits; capacity crowds; and major success. Much of that is captured in this celebration of City's stadia.

OUR FIRST GAME

By Gary James

Maine Road's opening game, against Sheffield United on August 23, 1923 was eagerly anticipated and was perceived as one of the most significant days in Manchester's history. News of the stadium's development had excited Mancunians and on August 21, the *Manchester Evening News* provided invaluable information on how to get to the new ground: "The first gate is sure to reach enormous proportions... Probably two-thirds of the crowd will wish to journey to their Mecca by tram car, and many of them are wondering how to do it."

The article went on to describe each of the main tram routes to the stadium and revealed plans that were being made to lay new tracks to allow multiple trams to load and unload at the same time. The opening game was treated in a similar manner to a major cup final with the local authority working with City and the tramways department to plan for transporting supporters from the city centre and, in particular, east Manchester, to the stadium.

Back then, club games were never all-ticket, with fans being able to decide at the last minute to pay to attend. This meant that no one knew how many would turn up. Plans were made for a figure of between 40,000 and over 80,000. The opening of Old Trafford in February 1910 could not be used as a guide, as a crowd of almost 45,000 watched Liverpool beat United 4-3. That crowd was little more than the official capacity of Hyde Road.

No matter how many people actually attended, it was clear the opening of Maine Road would be a major moment in the history of Manchester. Newspapers talked of how this would overshadow all other football that weekend. The *Manchester Evening News* explained: "In the First Division there is only one game between two local rivals, and that is Birmingham where Aston Villa will visit the St. Andrew's ground, but big as the attendance is, it is not likely to be as large as that seen on Manchester City's new ground at Moss Side, the opening of which is the chief event of the day."

The Main Stand under construction

The newspaper was correct as the Birmingham derby could only manage a crowd of 41,300. The article went on to stress the size of City's development: "That this vast stadium should have been practically completed between April 24 and August 24 of this year is the subject for wonder and admiration. It unquestionably creates a record in building construction, and it is a splendid testimonial to the organising powers of the contractors, Sir Robert McAlpine & Sons.

"Most people were freely sceptical as to whether the enclosure would be ready for tomorrow. A month ago it did not seem possible that it could be, but by the employment of hundreds of skilled workmen all but the internal work on the huge stand has been completed, and even this remaining task will not occupy more than a fortnight. The enclosure will accommodate well over 80,000 spectators."

Max Woosnam, a great all-round sports star and amateur footballer, was given the honour of captaining the Blues for this first match. Woosnam had suffered a broken leg which had limited his appearances for over a year and his return as captain was a fitting tribute. His injury had not only deprived him of a year in football, it also prevented him from defending his Wimbledon Doubles title won in 1921. He must have been immensely proud to lead the first City side into the new stadium.

The *Evening News* boasted that the day would be a proud moment in "the history of the City's premier football club", although not all Mancunians were convinced the move would be a good one.

Expressing similar sentiments to those 80 years later when City moved from Maine Road, supporter Harry Hughes was typical of many fans who felt the unique City atmosphere wouldn't be matched at this modern concrete bowl of a stadium: "When they moved to Maine Road I thought it wouldn't be popular. None of us did!" he said.

Max Woosnam introduces the Lord Mayor to the City team ahead of Maine Road's first match

"But we had to accept it. We were all so sad about it at the time, even though Maine Road was the last word in ground design. Hyde Road was home – it was City's ground and had grown with the club – and we loved it despite its appearance. United fans used to say that Old Trafford was better than Hyde Road. They'd say, 'You can see at Old Trafford!' and we'd respond, 'Well there's not many people in your way.' They didn't get big crowds then!"

Harry's fears about the atmosphere soon disappeared: "Even though it wasn't our real home the atmosphere was there and we quickly turned it into City's home. Hyde Road became a thing of the past, never forgotten, but rarely missed."

The *Manchester Guardian*'s report of the opening painted a powerful picture: "By one o'clock on Saturday the football march to Manchester City's new ground was in full swing. To a cricket match, unless it be a very important one or holds the prospect of an exciting finish, men walk easily and with an air of leisure, but to a football match they march like an army, with a set purpose in their minds and the ferment of the excitement to come already moving them. By one way or another 60,000 of them went to the new ground on Saturday and watched a fast and lively game. This ground is the last word in provision of comfort and security for and against the explosive force of the great crowds that follow the League teams.

"There is something almost barbaric in the impression which, when it is full, it makes on the observer. As one comes on it suddenly from Claremont Road, a great rounded embankment towers up in front, and over it at one side looms the highly arched roof of a stand whose dim recesses cannot be discerned at all except from the ground level... The topmost section sits aloof and remote at an incredible distance from the field. Like a squall falling suddenly from the hills, its clapping came at times in sudden gusts from far away."

The programme for the first match highlighted that it was: "A memorable day in the history of the club... Today marks an epoch in our history. For the first time we have a ground worthy of the club." The article commented that the club had decided to call the venue 'Maine-road'.

Maine Road's opening game was covered extensively. There were national film crews and reporters present. The main reports featured descriptions of the stadium, not the football. From what can be gathered it was an amazing game however. Sheffield United's goalkeeper, Gough, was replaced by outfield player Pantling after 30 minutes, and the new 'keeper immediately faced a penalty taken by Frank Roberts. Pantling saved the shot – causing Roberts to enter the record books as the first man to miss a penalty at Maine Road.

Whether the unusual surroundings impacted City isn't clear, but the Blues had been quite lethargic in the first half. *The Guardian* claimed: "In the second half Manchester City woke up and, after an even interval, were much the more aggressive. They got an excellent goal after a centre from the right wing, and another immediately afterwards when the left wing was allowed to dribble right in to the goal posts and put the ball across the mouth. But it is idle to pretend that the game mattered much on Saturday, except it was right that so great a crowd, so finely housed, should have taken so excellent a show to entertain them. May there be many such."

The Guardian also considered the age of the players and their descriptions make interesting reading today: "The game was good league football, played on the happiest green turf and fought as hardly and well as though the game had never stopped in April. There were few really young men on either side, but in athletics the day for youth and grace seems to have gone for the time. In cricket and football experience and stamina count for as much, and football runs to weight and 'build' and heavy shoulders.

Billy Austin, George Hicks, Tommy Johnson, Sam Cookson and Harry Roberts in training. The latter three all played in Maine Road's first game

Action from the historic encounter with Sheffield United, with the Popular Side in the background. Inset is the matchday programme for the day

"There can never have been so many half-bald heads as there are now, and the veterans hold their own. The only sign of the beginning of the season was that the players were not quite so melodramatic as they will be when the crowd's blood is up, though when a corner is to be taken there seems always to be six captains on one side and half a dozen on the other, and the extravagance with which a team throws itself on the colleague who has happened to score a goal would bring a blush to the cheek of the average schoolboy, that admirable standard of reserve."

The Blues actually won 2-1 with the historic first goal scored by Horace Barnes after about 68 minutes. Legendary striker Tommy Johnson netted the second, while Sheffield United's Harry Johnson pulled a goal back two minutes from time, thus providing the Blues with their first Maine Road victory.

Film of the ground's opening appeared in cinemas that week and it was claimed the attendance was an incredible 80,000. For many years the attendance has been written as anything from about 56,000 upwards but on August 31, 1923 the club formally announced that the official attendance was 58,159. The club confirmed that the figure included everybody present as, back then, figures usually excluded season ticket holders, whether they attended or not.

The opening game was the start of an amazing period for the club in which the capacity of Maine Road allowed City to flourish. Within a season the club had established the record crowd for any fixture at a club ground and then in 1927/28 City were once more the best supported club in the entire League. This was an amazing feat, as that was a second-tier season.

Five years after the move the *History of the Lancashire Football Association* was published. One section focused on City and, with the stadium still in its infancy, the book considered City's move: "The club now boasts a ground with the largest holding capacity outside Wembley, and with room for further extension and addition that could make the holding capacity of Wembley seem insignificant."

100
MAINE
Road
MEMORIES

A century on from the start of City's love
affair with Maine Road, we round up a
selection of moments, memories and people
that encapsulate the grand old stadium

1
CHARLES SWAIN
The architect

Maine Road's architect was Charles Swain (pictured right). Prior to City most of his work had focused on designing theatres and cinemas. His appointment as the new stadium's architect was a major show of faith in him and he created an arena that was the envy of football. His designs were so impressive that those planning the Scottish rugby stadium at Murrayfield came to Maine Road to view his work. Ultimately, Murrayfield's design was based on Maine Road with one large Main Stand surrounded by terracing when it was opened in 1925.

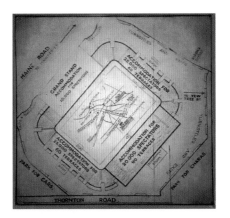

2
LAWRENCE FURNISS
The chairman

Lawrence Furniss (left) was the club's chairman responsible for the move to Maine Road in 1923. He was such an important figure that some fans had wanted the new stadium to be named after him. It is believed Furniss himself rejected the idea as he held the view that no individual should be given such a honour. Furniss had been a player with Gorton in the 1880s; secretary-manager of Ardwick when the club first joined the league; a director and he was the City president when City won the league in 1937. An often forgotten but truly important man.

Not at Maine Road but an action shot from Meredith's last season. This was a FA Cup tie at Brighton that City won 5-1 in February 1924. Meredith scored his last competitive goal that day

3
BILLY MEREDITH
The oldest player

Billy Meredith was the oldest player ever to appear at Maine Road at 49 years 238 days. Here he is (below) training during the stadium's first season of 1923/24, when he made his final appearance.

George Smith, seen here in front of the Main Stand, scored his five in a league game against Newport County on June 14, 1947. The game ended 5-1 on what was the latest finish to a season until the Covid pandemic delayed the 2019/20 season

4
MOST GOALS SCORED IN A GAME
Five-goal trio

Only three players scored five in a game at Maine Road – Tommy Browell, Frank Roberts and George Smith.

Tommy Browell, who scored five in the league game with Burnley on October 24, 1925 (an 8-3 City win)

Frank Roberts' five came in a FA Cup tie against Crystal Palace on February 20, 1926 (City won 11-4)

One of the Popular Side tunnels can be seen above goalkeeper Len Langford's back in this image from a 2-2 draw with Everton in September 1933

5
THE TUNNELS
Crowd control

When Maine Road was constructed plans were adapted after the 1923 FA Cup final, which had seen major issues with crowd control. Architect Charles Swain decided to add additional exits, so huge tunnels in each corner, and in both the Popular Side (Kippax) and Maine Stand, were planned.

The same tunnel can be seen here in 1969 during a training session featuring goalkeeper Joe Corrigan

Billy Walsh in 1947 with the corner tunnel between the Main Stand and the Scoreboard End (later North Stand) in the background

6
84,569!
The record crowd

In 1924 Maine Road established the record crowd for any game at a club ground and outside of London. That was 76,166 for the visit of Cardiff but a decade later Maine Road eclipsed that record with a new one that still stands today. The City v Stoke FA Cup tie of March 1934 was watched by an incredible 84,569. This newspaper cutting (right) shows the only goal of the game, scored by Eric Brook (the figure in the distance near the Popular Side/ Kippax terracing).

THE WAY TO WEMBLEY
BROOK'S AMAZING SHOT BEAT STOKE

STOP PRESS NEWS

Here's the squad from 1935/36, pictured in front of the Main Stand. Back (left to right): Tom Chorlton (trainer), Jackie Bray, Billy Dale, Robert Donnelly, Frank Swift, Matt Busby, Sam Barkas, Laurie Barnett (Assistant trainer) D Sinclair (Assistant Secretary). Sitting: Alec Herd, Jim Cassidy, Fred Tilson, Wilf Wild (Secretary / Manager), Bobby Marshall, Jack Percival, Billy Owen. Ground: Ernie Toseland, Eric Brook. Brook scored in the 1-1 draw with Arsenal

7
RECORD LEAGUE ATTENDANCE
Another record crowd

City's record league attendance of 79,491 was set v Arsenal on February 23, 1935. At the time this was a record for the entire Football League.

8
CELEBRATORY PITCH INVASIONS
Sharing in the joy

There were many celebratory pitch invasions over the years at Maine Road. In 1937 when City won the league title for the first time after the game with Sheffield Wednesday, fans poured on to the field to congratulate the players. Similar scenes occurred after every major success at the ground, whether it be a celebration of achieving promotion, winning a major trophy or of reaching a significant final.

Manager Wilf Wild with the Football League trophy after City triumphed in 1937

City fans run on to the pitch to celebrate the 5-2 aggregate victory over Schalke in 1970 that meant the club had reached its first European final

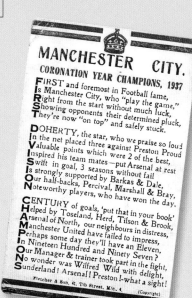

9
TITLE SUCCESS
The first of many...

City's first league title came in 1936/37 after a 4-1 home win against Sheffield Wednesday on April 24, 1937. These images are pages from the match programme for that match. The key game for many had come two weeks earlier when City defeated Arsenal 2-0 at Maine Road. This was perceived as the title decider but in the end Arsenal dropped to third place with City winning the title by three points from second-placed Charlton.

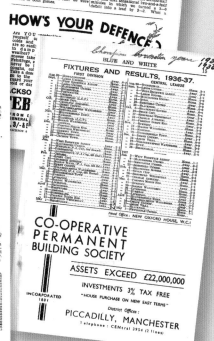

10
OTHER SPORTS AT MAINE ROAD
The sporting venue

A variety of other sports were played at Maine Road over the years including tennis and rugby. The rugby league championship play-off was staged there in 1939 and then from 1946 to 1956, with the 1949 game between Huddersfield and Warrington watched by 75,194.

Tennis at Maine Road in 1939...

WORLD TENNIS STARS
Spectacular Series of Matches
SINGLES AND DOUBLES

At the
MANCHESTER CITY F.C.
GROUND, MAINE ROAD
JULY 14 and 15
Friday 5-45 • Saturday 3-0

DONALD BUDGE
BILL TILDEN
ELLSWORTH VINES
LESTER STOEFEN

Official Programme Price 2d.

Warrington defeated Oldham 7-3 in the championship play-off final held in 1955, watched by 49,434. The Warrington captain Albert Naughton is chaired off the field holding the league championship trophy after the match

ENGLAND. 8. SCOTLAND. 0.
at Maine Road, Manchester. 16th October. 1943.
War International Match.

SCOTLAND'S SUPREME HUMILIATION

NEVER has a Scottish Soccer team been so humiliated as that at Maine-road, Manchester, yesterday, when an 8-0 margin for England was a true indication of how the game went. Indeed, the winners' total should have been nine, but a penalty kick was missed by Carter.

By ALF. CLARKE

Cullis   *Lawton*

Scotland had five newcomers to international football, and while one cannot lay the blame on them individually, the team as a whole played with a complete lack of understanding. If the Tartan selectors cannot discover a better team than this the game north of the Tweed must be on the poverty line.

It is hard to know whether to praise England or feel sorry for Scotland, for it is many years since I saw a team and any description in senior football so outclassed.

Brilliant Half-backs

Swift, the Manchester City goalkeeper, might never have been there at all. He certainly had good saves from Gillick and Waddell, and he never saw a shot from Dougan that hit the crossbar, but those represented the sum total of Scotland's shooting power.

Soo and Hardwick in defence were never extended, though Deakin did occasionally trouble the Arsenal man.

It was, however, the brilliant work of the half-backs which enabled England to take full toll.

Cullis played a captain's part in every detail. Mirren centre-forward never had a sage rush, but the Scottish Mercer, were guilty in every sense of the word. The former also got a right back on Walker, who was occasionally flashed into prominence.

To Scotland thought Miller, the Celtic player installed at left back, could save the Matthews problem they were grossly mistaken.

The manner scintillating form, and Miller has gone the same way as the rest. That means that there is not a full-back in the game who can hold Matthews.

Carter made him a cunning partner; Lawton was always dangerous.

Hagan played grandly throughout, and Compton made up a dazzling forward line.

It was accomplished so easily and so unhurried.

For Scotland, Crozier, one of the new newcomers, improved as the game went on—his fielding of the ball was never clean.

Carbine struggled heroically, and if Little started more as the game wore on. Young did not have a good match—and Campion was not confident.

But over the forwards it is best to draw a veil.

Waddell and Walker cannot look back with any satisfaction upon his win, too good work at times, was never so good, and Deakin, thought dangerous as one would expect from a virtuoso.

England's scorers were: Lawton (4), Matthews (2), Carter, and Hagan. It was a great success, being a five.

There was and the rec...

England's record victory over Scotland —By ARTHUR SHRIVE

England   8   Scotland

AFTER the match at Maine-road, Manchester, a Scot said to me, "Remember, these Englishmen have been playing together so long that they are almost like a club side. We have not had the same opportunity of developing team work."

It is true that in recent seasons the England selectors have been able to call on highly-skilled players, and not found it necessary to make many changes.

In this game England rose to the heights, and gave a display of fast, virile and constructive football such as the 60,000 spectators at £10,000 had not seen for a long time. Since the two countries first met in 1872 there surely cannot have been a more one-sided game, and the victory was the most decisive in the whole series, though this match will not go down in the records as a full international.

A HOPELESS CAUSE

In the early part of the game the Scottish forwards showed glimpses of their native craft, but before long England had taken full control, and for the rest the Scots laboured on a hopeless cause. They were plucky but outclassed. Their half-backs were over-run and the defence torn wide open.

Though beaten eight times—five the first half—Crozier, the Brentford goalkeeper – one of the five new comers in the side – made many fine saves, including a penalty taken by Carter, who shot wide when the ball came back to him. Carabine struggled hard at right back, and Walker and Deakin on the left wing were the only forwards to catch the occasionally.

The return of Lawton as leader of the England forwards proved a great success. His touches and deft touches and scored four with...

War International Match.

—And this is Matthews (No. 7) scoring goal No. 8

England 8. Scotland 0.   By HENRY ROSE

A GATE of 60,000 paid £10,600 to see England whip the Scots by a record international score in Manchester yesterday.

If players were paid on their entertainment-value £10,000 of that sum should be distributed among the England players.

They gave us sheer magic and proved themselves the best England team seen for many years.

Some of their movements were almost impudent and at times they had Scotland so bewildered that they could fall down, get up, and then beat their man

Five in...

take him, and woe to Scotland, neither did they.

Thank you, Stan, and thanks, too, to the other Stanley—Cullis, the English captain, who stamped his dominating personality on the game almost from the first kick.

Cullis was assertive, strident, the soul of urgency, getting the big jobs done quickly with singleness of... and purpose.

...rest of the England team... nothing but bouquets in...

...goals came in this order:
...from a cute back heel
...wton.
..., a header from a per-... placed free kick by
...from a lovely back pass
...gan.
..., an acrobatic overhead
...he lay on the ground
... how he I did it." he
...erwards.
...from a perfect pass by
...s.
...and after Carter had
...alty, came
...fter a brilliant solo
...ercer
...rom a long throw-out
...without a Scot touch-
...
...—and just what the
...ed—after a wonder-
... drawing the biggest
...me

Football League North
Cup. Qualifying Round.
MANCHESTER CITY. 0.
OLDHAM ATHLETIC. 0.
at Maine Rd, Manchester.
8th January 1944.

Sproston Best Forward

MANCHESTER CITY and Oldham played a goalless draw at Maine Road and it was a true reflex of the game (writes Alf. Clarke).

On two occasions McDowall and Paton struck the crossbar, and Sproston was once clean through only to shoot straight at the goalkeeper. Sproston, however, was City's best forward at inside right.

The City international right back did some grand work but the City line was not so well balanced, although the defence played well.

Oldham's attack faded out after the interval, Wornall was the pick, and Gray played a grand game at centre half-back.

EIGHT goals were fired into the Scottish net in the International with England at Manchester City's ground yesterday. Here is the fourth—by Lawton (Everton) on the ground. Scots' consolation is that this top score of all these tests does not count in the records—it was only a war-time game and therefore "unofficial."

11
INTERNATIONAL FOOTBALL: ENGLAND v SCOTLAND
Rivals reunited

In October 1943, a wartime morale-boosting international was staged between Scotland and England at Maine Road that resulted in a comprehensive win for the English side. With City's Frank Swift in nets and future City manager Joe Mercer playing, England defeated Scotland 8-0 in front of 60,000. Tommy Lawton netted four but Stanley Matthews was acclaimed as the man of the match by many attending. These newspaper cuttings are taken from the scrapbook of City fan Dennis Chapman, who was there that day.

A City official keeps an eye on the fans at the September 1947 home derby. The attendance that day, recorded as over 78,000 by the club, is the largest for a Manchester derby outside of Wembley

City captain Bert Sproston (left) and United's Johnny Carey at Maine Road before the September 1947 derby, which ended goalless

George Smith with United's Johnny Carey during a Maine Road derby in 1947/48

12
AWAY AT HOME
City played Utd 'away' at Maine Road

Following the bombing of Old Trafford's Main Stand during the war, City offered United the use of Maine Road for games. This meant that sometimes City would be the away team at Maine Road for derby matches. According to former City player George Smith when looking back on this era during the stadium's final season, City always got to the ground early to make sure they had the home dressing room.

Roy Clarke, Jack Oakes, Joe Fagan, Dennis Westcott and George Smith in the home dressing room bath

Evening Chronicle

Souvenir Picture of Manchester City

THE MEN WHO WON PROMOTION

(May, 1947)

STANDING (left to right): L. Barnett (trainer), Sam Cowan (manager), Percival, Sproston, Black, Fagan, Swift, Constantine, Westwood, Emptage, Williams, Wilf Wild (secretary), F. Tilson (assistant trainer) ; SITTING (left to right) : Dunkley, Smith, Barkas (captain), Wharton, Walsh ; INSET : (left) Herd ; (right) McDowall.

13
RECORD DIVISIONAL ATTENDANCE
Biggest Division 2 crowd

When City defeated Burnley in 1947, it attracted almost 70,000 to Maine Road. The official attendance was 69,463 and this was a record for a Second Division match at the time. City and Burnley were both fighting for promotion that day with City winning the Second Division title. Burnley would ultimately finish second, four points behind the Blues.

Here's Frank Swift during the 1947/48 season with the Popular Side (later Kippax) in the background

14
42,725
Not just average

Within four years of moving to Maine Road, City became the most popular side in the entire Football League. They had first achieved the feat back at Hyde Road in 1910/11 and again in 1914/15, but the ground struggled to cope with crowds over 30,000. Once City moved to Maine Road crowds could increase and in 1927/28 City attracted 37,468, which was the highest in the league. An impressive feat, especially as City were a Second Division club at the time. The following season they were the best supported club again. The highest average attendance ever achieved by City while at Maine Road came 20 years later when the Blues attracted an average of 42,725 in 1947/48.

15
TRAUTMANN'S SAVES
Wunderbar German

Legendary goalkeeper Bert Trautmann thrilled fans with many incredible performances from the late 1940s to early 1960s. He's pictured above in full flight as he leaps across to stop an effort on goal during the goalless First Division match against Wolverhampton Wanderers in August 1951, watched by 45,849. Notice the City flag (above) and the fans on the Popular Side.

Trautmann gets his fingertips to the ball watched by Meadows (our number 2) and Chelsea's Bentley (9) in September 1954. The game ended 1-1

16
FLOODLIT MATCH
Let there be lights

Maine Road's first floodlit matches came in 1953 when the club installed its first permanent set of lights. To mark the occasion, the Blues organised celebratory floodlit midweek games against Hearts (a 6-3 win on October 14), Fenerbahce (a 5-1 win on October 21) and Celtic (a 1-1 draw on October 28). For the Hearts match the players wore a special shiny, satin shirt which it was hoped would add to the spectacle.

Maine Road's second set of floodlights used to be referenced in a chant by United fans who claimed that City having 'the tallest floodlights' was one of our boasts in the days when City were less successful on the pitch than the Reds. Leeds actually had the tallest lights, but that fact was lost on our rivals! Here's one in March 1982 as City defeat West Bromwich Albion 2-1

Manchester United take on Charlton Athletic at Maine Road in August 1947. Sam Bartram, Charlton's legendary goalkeeper, runs out to save from Charlie Mitten in the first minute of the game

European action under the Maine Road floodlights between United and Bilbao, February 1957

17
GOOD NEIGHBOURS
Lighting up Europe

Manchester United had two spells at Maine Road. The first followed Old Trafford's bombing during the war when the Reds played home games at City from 1941 to 1949. The second came during 1956/57 when United played European games there.

At the time, Old Trafford did not have floodlights. Many Blues would attend these matches, helping United attract 75,598 for the visit of Borussia Dortmund. As of 2023, this is still United's highest home attendance in Europe.

18
THE CITY FLAG
Flying high

For decades there was a flag that flew at Maine Road that was loved by the fans. In City blue and white it simply read 'City F.C'. with the top half white lettering on blue and the bottom being blue letters on white. The flag was a regular sight on the Popular Side, becoming the Kippax, and when that was roofed it was moved to the Scoreboard End. Here it is in 1958. It disappeared in the 1960s when fans of Liverpool are alleged to have captured it.

Glyn Pardoe played a significant part in City's successes later in the decade and here he is with other members of the squad as they prepare for the visit of Spurs in December 1967. Left to right: Tony Book, Tony Coleman, Mike Doyle, Colin Bell, George Heslop, Francis Lee, Dave Connor, Glyn Pardoe, Ken Mulhearn, Neil Young, Alan Oakes and Mike Summerbee

19
GLYN PARDOE'S DEBUT
The youngest player

Glyn Pardoe is the youngest City player ever
to play a first-team game and he made his debut
on April 11, 1962 in a 4-1 defeat by Birmingham
City at Maine Road. At the time he was 15 years
and 314 days old.

Glyn Pardoe sitting at the kitchen table as his mother pours him a cup
of tea on the day of the game against Birmingham City in 1962

20
THE MOSAICS
A City identity

Local children (pictured left) playing football in September 1962 beneath one of three mosaics built into the Main Stand frontage. There were two semi-circular ones like this which lasted from 1923 through to the stadium's demolition, as well as a rectangular one above the main entrance that became damaged in the 1970s.

The Manchester City sign gets a coat of paint in 1991

The central mosaic photographed in 1963

21
ROYAL VISITS
King, club and country

From 1920 when King George V
attended a City victory over Liverpool
at Hyde Road through to the modern
era, royalty have often paid visits to
Manchester City. Maine Road had the
pleasure of welcoming the future King
George VI (then known as the Duke of
York) to a game with Derby in 1934
and in 1964 Prince Philip (Queen
Elizabeth II's husband) watched a
Manchester derby. Here he chats
with City's directors in front of the
1934 FA Cup-winning team photo.

Trautmann leads out the combined Manchester City and Manchester United team against an All-Star International XI, wearing City's away kit of the period, led by Jimmy Armfield in April 1964

22
TRAUTMANN'S TESTIMONIAL
47,000 and the rest

In 1964 thousands were locked out of Maine Road as City staged a testimonial for Bert Trautmann. Officially there were more than 47,000 there but those present that night believe the attendance easily exceeded 60,000.

The champagne is flowing as Bill Foulkes (far left), Denis Law, Derek Kevan, Bobby Charlton and Maurice Setters toast Bert. Below is Trautmann against Spurs at Maine Road circa 1961

Here's Mercer, Allison and the squad at the beginning of the 1965/66 Second Division campaign. Back row, left to right: Mike Summerbee, Neil Young, Cliff Sear, Dave Bacuzzi, Mike Doyle, George Heslop, Alan Oakes. Next row: Malcolm Allison, Harry Dowd, Alan Ogley, Dave Ewing. Third row: Johnny Hart, Bobby Kennedy, Glyn Pardoe, physio Peter Blakey. Second row: Dave Connor, Johnny Crossan. Front Joe Mercer

Johnny Crossan, Joe Mercer and Harry Godwin celebrate promotion in 1966. Groundsman Stan Gibson is in the background with the trophy lid on his head!

23
PROMOTION
Mercer's first managerial success at City

In 1965 Joe Mercer became the manager of City and he recruited Malcolm Allison as his assistant. The following five years brought immense success to the club and helped resurrect the Blues. Over those seasons they won the league, the FA Cup, the League Cup and the club's first major European trophy. However, it all started with the Second Division title in 1966.

24
THE ORIGINAL SOUVENIR SHOP
Any spares?

This building (pictured left) was City's new ticket office in August 1966 but those who remember Maine Road from the 1970s to 1990s may recall this more as the club's souvenir shop. Every time the building had a new use the club seemed to quickly outgrow it. A new ticket office was constructed when the North Stand was built between 1971 and 1973, with this building then becoming the club's first permanent shop. It was tiny! It was positioned next to the Social Club and in the mid-1990s the much larger building was converted into the club's new store. This building then became an office for the Junior Blues and other staff and remained an office until the demolition of Maine Road in 2004.

25
CORONATION STREET AT MAINE ROAD
Screen stars watch on

In November 1967, Coronation Street viewers were treated to the sight of several characters attending a game at Maine Road as part of a storyline. The idea was that Rovers Return landlady Annie Walker wanted to attend a game on the terraces at City to see what it was like. Ultimately she is caught in possession of a toilet roll and is arrested, assumed to be a football hooligan (it was a typical 1960s storyline!). Much of the episode was filmed at Maine Road on matchday with Annie Walker joining Jerry Booth, Stan Ogden, Len Fairclough and Lucille Hewitt on the Scoreboard End for an actual game.

26
THE BALLET ON ICE
Quick, quick, snow

This became a real Maine Road classic as Tottenham were defeated 4-1 in the heavy snow in December 1967. Many felt the game should have been postponed but City were keen to prove what they were capable of. The match became known as the 'Ballet on Ice' due to the grace and poise displayed by the City team on a tricky surface. Colin Bell, Mike Summerbee, Tony Coleman and Neil Young were the scorers for the Blues.

27
THE SCOREBOARD END
What's the score?

Years before electronic scoreboards, Maine Road had its own scoreboard hut, positioned appropriately enough, at the Scoreboard End (later North Stand). Each letter would correspond with a fixture printed in the match programme and during the game staff would put numbers up against the letters to show the scores at those matches. This photo (left) captures the moment on October 28, 1967 just after Colin Bell had scored the only goal of the Division One match with Leeds.

28
EUROPEAN FIRST
No Turkish delight

It was the first taste of European Cup competition for City at Maine Road in 1968 but this first leg game with Turkish team Fenerbahce ended goalless. The Blues went out after losing the second leg 2-1 – the result was regarded as the greatest European victory in Turkish football history at the time.

Fenerbahce goalkeeper Simsek Yavuz being chaired off the pitch by Turkish supporters and officials after the Maine Road encounter

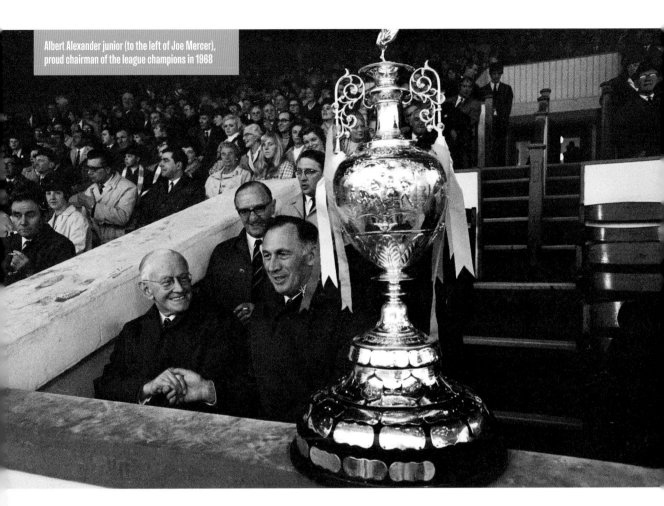

Albert Alexander junior (to the left of Joe Mercer), proud chairman of the league champions in 1968

29
THE ALEXANDERS
The great family

Throughout Maine Road's life as a football ground, members of the Alexander family were significant figures at the club. Albert Alexander senior was involved with City from 1894 and became vice-chairman. He also acted as caretaker-manager from November 1925 through to April 1926. His son Albert junior was the chairman when Joe Mercer brought City major success in the 1960s and 1970s. Albert junior's son Eric was himself chairman of the club in the early 1970s and a honorary president by the time of Maine Road's demolition.

Albert senior (far right) introducing the City team to King George V at the 1934 FA Cup final at Wembley

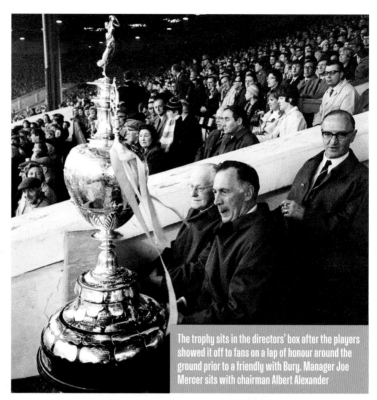

30
THE LEAGUE TITLE
Champions again

Newly-crowned champions City show off the league championship trophy to fans after its presentation at Maine Road in 1968 (above), while Tony Book holds the trophy aloft in front of the Platt Lane Stand (below).

The trophy sits in the directors' box after the players showed it off to fans on a lap of honour around the ground prior to a friendly with Bury. Manager Joe Mercer sits with chairman Albert Alexander

31
MALCOLM ALLISON
The big coach

Malcolm Allison was a larger than life character who was loved by fans during his time as assistant manager to Joe Mercer from 1965. He helped City to major success domestically and in Europe. A supremely talented coach who was at his best at Maine Road.

Allison at Maine Road in 1969

Stan Gibson in front of the North Stand

32
STAN GIBSON
The groundsman

Stan Gibson was
City's groundsman
for over 40 years.
He lived in one of the
club houses on Maine
Road (see next page)
and saw the stadium's
pitch as his garden. Woe
betide any player or
manager who wanted
to put extra hours in
training while Stan
was groundsman.

Stan with the FA Cup in 1969

33
THE CLUB HOUSES
Home from home

Next door to Maine Road were two houses owned by the club. Over the years, players and club officials lived in these properties. For example, in the 1920s captain Jimmy McMullan lived in one. For the last 40 years of the stadium's life the main occupant was groundsman Stan Gibson and by the time this photograph (above) was taken during the ground's final season, both houses (seen here from the side, on the right) were used as club offices and store rooms.

Here Stan Gibson's daughter Janice is seen in their back garden with the FA Cup. Notice the stadium floodlights in the background

34
ALAN OAKES' RECORD
The most appearances

Alan Oakes played more games at Maine Road than anyone else (341). He's also City's record appearance holder, and is pictured below in 1970.

Alan Oakes in action v Southampton, October 1970

35
AWAY COLOURS AT HOME
The shirt changes

Although it seems unusual today, there were many times over the decades that City wore 'away' colours at Maine Road. Fans often talk of a couple of games against Tottenham in the 1980s when the referee decided that Spurs' white was too close to City's pale blue, forcing City to change into their second strip. In past decades, wearing away colours in FA Cup games and other competitions at home was more of a regular occurrence.

City in their second strip of red and black stripes face Chelsea in the semi-final of the European Cup Winners' Cup at Maine Road in April 1971. Goalkeeper Ron Healey is under pressure from Chelsea's Keith Weller. Note the North Stand being constructed in the background

36
BLUE MOBILITY CARS PITCHSIDE
Car corner

This may be an image of Colin Bell in a classic City kit (left) but look into the distance and you'll see the blue Invacar vehicles that were a regular feature at grounds around the country. The cars were created to help people with disabilities drive and many clubs allowed the drivers to bring their vehicles into the ground and position them close to the touchline. This photo was taken in August 1971 and the vehicles are positioned in the Kippax/Platt Lane corner.

37
THE SOCIAL CLUB
Fun and festivities

Opened in 1966, the Manchester City Social Club was the heartbeat of the club for years. This image (right) shows the interior in August 1970 after it had been extended with a new bar and restaurant.

Every year the Social Club would stage the club's pantomime. Here are Mike Summerbee, Tony Book, Francis Lee and Joe Corrigan, who were appearing in Aladdin in December 1971

Future City manager Alan Ball, then an Arsenal player, is being watched by (left to right) Alan Oakes, Tony Towers and Mike Doyle

38
CITY v ARSENAL
The most league games

Arsenal played more league games against City at Maine Road than any other team – meeting on a total of 56 occasions. The images on this page are all taken from a March 1972 encounter.

Alan Oakes (left) and Willie Donachie (far right) watch Tony Towers take the ball from Alan Ball with the Platt Lane Stand in the background

The referee has a few words with Mike Summerbee in that same game

COLIN THE KING
The most goals at Maine Road

Colin Bell scored more goals for City at Maine Road than any other player – 107 first-team strikes in total.

Here 'King Colin', as he was described in the newspapers the next day, is mobbed by Rodney Marsh, Colin Barrett and Mike Doyle as he scores City's third goal from an incredibly tight angle against Manchester United in November 1972. The Blues won the game 3-0 in front of 52,086

40
MARSH'S DEBUT
The major transfer

In March 1972 Rodney Marsh signed for City in a highly-publicised transfer. He made his debut against Chelsea later that month in front of 53,322 at Maine Road.

Here secretary Walter Griffiths checks the paperwork in front of manager Malcolm Allison and chairman Eric Alexander in the City boardroom

Eric takes Rodney for a walk around the ground. The newly-constructed North Stand is in the background. In the close season, grey plastic seats would be added to that terracing to make it an all-seater stand

41
'LOOK AT HIS FACE...'
The famous line

One of the most famous phrases in commentary was uttered by the BBC broadcaster Barry Davies when former Blue hero Francis Lee netted the winner for Derby County at the Platt Lane end of the ground in 1974. It was a brilliant strike from some distance and made the score 2-1 but it's Davies' commentary that is remembered most by football fans. "Interesting, very interesting..." then Davies adds: "Look at his face, just look at his face" as Lee celebrated arms aloft. In September 2004 Davies announced he was retiring from football commentary and his final game was City v Arsenal that month. City boss Kevin Keegan presented him with this signed shirt on behalf of the club.

42
THE MAIN ENTRANCE 'CAGE'
Tight security

In the early 1970s, after some vandalism and attempted break-ins, the main entrance was remodelled with a cage to protect the actual door. Here is Denis Law leaving the players' entrance at Maine Road, positioned next to the cage, on the day he retired – August 26, 1974.

Here's Helen at Wembley in 1976 celebrating the League Cup triumph with Joe Corrigan, Mike Doyle and her famous bell

43
HELEN TURNER'S BELL
Ringing in the glory

Helen Turner was a popular presence at Maine Road for decades. She used to bring a bell to the game with her, and from the '70s to the stadium's final day she was a regular in the North Stand, close to the goal.

44
COLIN BELL'S RETURN
Hero's comeback

On Boxing Day 1977, City's legendary England international Colin Bell returned to action after half-time in the game with Newcastle. The midfielder had been injured in the November 1975 Manchester derby and, despite a brief return at the end of that season, had been fighting a long battle to regain fitness. His return against Newcastle was one of the most emotional nights ever experienced at Maine Road, with City winning 4-0.

Colin poses at Maine Road with the North Stand in the background

Neil Young nets his second of the night in the 1970 Cup Winners' Cup semi-final second leg

45
EUROPEAN NIGHTS
Setting sights for glory

There were many memorable European nights at Maine Road with impressive victories over Milan (3-0 on December 6, 1978), Juventus (1-0, September 15, 1976) and many others but the game that is often remembered as the greatest European occasion at Maine Road was the 5-1 victory over Schalke on April 15, 1970. This was the second leg of the European Cup Winners' Cup semi-final and meant Joe Mercer's Blues won 5-2 on aggregate. They went on to beat Gornik in the final in Vienna.

46
THE BOARDROOM
The seats of power

In the 1970s the Maine Road boardroom was typical of most football clubs. There were a few pennants and trophies dotted around, some glassware, a central table and typical heaters of the period. This was City's boardroom during 1978/79 (right). The Blues had won the Central League (the main reserve league at the time) and the trophy is on the shelf closest to the door, adorned with blue and white ribbons. The boardroom remained like this until the mid-1990s when the entire floor was gutted and rebuilt as a hospitality area called the Boardroom Suite.

Bobby McDonald heads City's second against Everton with Dennis Tueart watching on from the far right

47
FA CUP QUARTER-FINAL v EVERTON
A great replayed victory for City

A 2-2 draw at Goodison Park in March 1981 earned City an FA Cup sixth-round replay at Maine Road. Following a goalless first half in Manchester, City took the lead thanks to Bobby McDonald's strike in the 65th minute. No sooner had the Blues celebrated, then McDonald headed the second, with Paul Power adding the third in 85th minute. Everton's consolation goal came from Peter Eastoe in the 89th minute. The attendance was 52,532, and City went on to Wembley after beating Ipswich Town 1-0 in the semi-final.

48
JOHN BOND'S FALL
Beaten and bruised

During his time as manager John Bond (pictured here with City chairman Peter Swales) would often watch the game from the directors' box at Maine Road. After City defeated Norwich 6-0 in the FA Cup fourth round on January 24, 1981, Bond injured himself as he jumped down from the directors' box to console his son, Norwich player (and future Blue) Kevin Bond.

49
MIDDLESBROUGH OR MAN UNITED?
Are you United in disguise?

When Middlesbrough arrived at Maine Road for their top-flight game with City in January 1981 they had no idea that the match would appear on television that weekend. In those days, though shirt sponsorship was allowed, teams could not wear a sponsor's name during a game shown on TV. The game scheduled for broadcast at Bolton was postponed and so the TV cameras were sent to Maine Road instead. Middlesbrough had arrived with shirts bearing their sponsor's name, so they sent someone over to Old Trafford to borrow a kit from United to play in. This meant that Middlesbrough played City in United shirts. The Blues beat the Reds 3-2 with goals from Tommy Hutchison, Bobby McDonald and Kevin Reeves.

Middlesbrough's David Hodgson became the first man to score wearing a United first-team shirt at Maine Road that season. In fact, Hodgson and Tony McAndrew were the ONLY men to score at Maine Road that season in a first-team game wearing United's colours!

50
SCOTLAND'S NUMBER ONE
Keeping it calm

When City faced Watford at the start of the 1982/83 season, goalkeeper Joe Corrigan was injured three minutes into the game and had to be substituted. Back then only one substitute was allowed and this would typically be an outfield player. This day it was Dennis Tueart who came on for the injured Corrigan with defender Bobby McDonald taking over in nets. What followed was a bizarre style of goalkeeping which fans loved. The ground frequently erupted with chants of 'Scotland's Number One' to McDonald, who helped City achieve a 1-0 victory. The goal was scored by substitute Tueart too.

An early 1990s view from the North Stand looking towards the 1935 Platt Lane Stand with the 1982 Main Stand roof on the right

51
THE BARRELLED ROOF
Underneath the arches

In 1981 City announced a major redevelopment of Maine Road with the intention that new roofs would be placed over the Main Stand and Kippax with a new Platt Lane Stand erected, designed to match the existing North Stand. In 1982 the first phase of the plan was completed when a white barrelled roof was installed. Executive boxes were to be added to that roof but relegation in 1983 meant that every part of the development plan was put on hold. Ultimately, it was never completed but the white roof became an iconic part of Maine Road during its final two decades.

A sad sight: the roof during demolition in 2004

The old roof being removed in 1982

The roof can be seen from the newly-constructed Kippax in 1995

This image from 1982/83 shows the forecourt view of the Main Stand and its roof

52
THE SCOREBOARD'S MISSING LETTERS
The digital age

In 1971 when the new North Stand opened, it had a state of the art electronic scoreboard built into the back of it. By the 1990s however this scoreboard seemed somewhat temperamental and words would often be incomprehensible. It can be seen here during 1983/84 (pictured above) when it was still functioning relatively well and often carried details of match sponsors, as well as football scores.

A day when the scoreboard had had enough. Look carefully. It's saying 'AAAAAAAAAAAAAAAA' as City drew 0-0 with Birmingham in 1982

53
THE WHITE WALL AND POLICE SEATS
The cheap seats

Surrounding the pitch on all sides from 1923 until the 1990s, when the new Platt Lane and Kippax Stands changed things, was a white perimeter wall. For fans it was a classic Maine Road sight. There were also blue wooden seats built into the wall, as seen during City's 2-1 victory over Arsenal in December 1982 (left), which were mostly used by police to monitor the crowd, though bizarrely they faced the pitch rather than the terraces. At least they had a good view of the football.

54
'TRUMANNS FOR STEEL' ADVERT BOARD
It was a sign!

The 'Trumanns For Steel' sign became a highly memorable advertising board for decades. So much so that fans replicated it at the Etihad in a banner. There were a few different boards over the years, with one positioned on the Main Stand roof for a time. This one is on the Kippax and can be seen during the City v Coventry game of October 1982 (pictured left). The City player in the tangle is Kevin Bond.

55
DEMONSTRATIONS
The change was coming

Back in the 1980s, particularly during the 1986/87 season, many games would end with a demonstration against the chairman Peter Swales and supporting directors. At the final whistle fans on the Kippax would rush around to the forecourt outside the main entrance chanting 'Swales out' and 'sack the board' as they pushed for change.

A demonstration from 1983 looking from the stadium towards Maine Road itself

56
LUTON '83
The heartbreak

The 1982/83 season ended with a shock relegation after the Blues were defeated 1-0 by Luton on the last day of the season (right and below). This was the first relegation many Blues had experienced and came only two years after an FA Cup final appearance. Future City boss Brian Horton captained Luton and the attendance was 42,843.

Tommy Caton in action with a packed Kippax behind

The North Stand and Kippax corner watch on. The City player is Kevin Bond as City are relegated

The sign, the Kippax and goalkeeper Alex Williams during the Sheffield Wednesday game in December 1983

'Welcome To Maine Road' on the Kippax roof, November 1982

57
WELCOME TO MAINE ROAD
A sign from above

The 'Welcome To Maine Road' sign on top of the Kippax Stand was a popular landmark at the ground for years. Here it is during the City v Sheffield Wednesday game of December 1983 (above), which was watched by 41,862 in the Second Division.

58
CROWD CONTROL
The Kippax fencing

For the first 50 years of Maine Road there was little in the way of segregation for supporters. Occasionally in the 1960s, terracing would be separated into areas for home and away fans by using ropes on the Kippax. Temporary barriers started to be added depending on the reputation of away fans. By the mid-1970s clubs gradually added fences and created permanent barriers to keep fans apart. The away section was divided into a back and front section and for some games City fans would have one of those sections, depending on the number of fans expected. Alex Williams is pictured (right) in front of the segregated fans in a shot from 1984.

Here's a view looking towards the segregation fence on the Kippax in the early 1990s. By the time this was taken the segregation 'no-go zone', which was manned by police, had doubled in width from its size in the 1980s

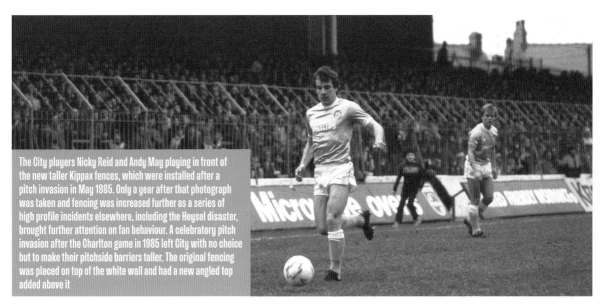

The City players Nicky Reid and Andy May playing in front of the new taller Kippax fences, which were installed after a pitch invasion in May 1985. Only a year after that photograph was taken and fencing was increased further as a series of high profile incidents elsewhere, including the Heysel disaster, brought further attention on fan behaviour. A celebratory pitch invasion after the Charlton game in 1985 left City with no choice but to make their pitchside barriers taller. The original fencing was placed on top of the white wall and had a new angled top added above it

Policemen on duty outside the Scoreboard End turnstiles, next to the Main Stand for the FA Cup semi-final match between Everton and Liverpool, March 1950

West Bromwich Albion's Jeff Astle celebrates scoring the opening goal in a FA Cup quarter-final second replay in April 1968. Note the second version of the Main Stand roof which had been altered two years earlier

59
NEUTRAL VENUE
The Maine Road to Wembley

Maine Road was often used as a neutral venue for major games, including the 1984 League Cup final replay and a variety of FA Cup third replays and semi-finals over the years.

The April 1973 FA Cup semi-final which saw Leeds United beat Wolverhampton Wanderers 1-0. Leeds keeper David Harvey saves a shot with Jack Charlton in support

Billy Bremner (not in picture) scores the only goal of the aforementioned 1973 FA Cup semi-final at Maine Road

Jim Melrose applauds the Blues fans from the Main Stand as City gained promotion in 1985

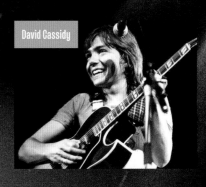

David Cassidy

60
CHARLTON '85
The promotion

After relegation in 1983, City took two seasons to return to football's top flight. Promotion came via a 5-1 victory over Charlton Athletic on May 11, 1985. The official crowd was 47,285 but those present that day believe there were at least another 10,000 packed into the stadium.

CONCERTS
The Maine music

The first concert staged at Maine Road was by teen heart-throb David Cassidy in May 1974, but it wasn't until the mid 1980s that the stadium hosted its next concert. That was Queen, supported by Status Quo, and from then on concerts became regular events at the old ground, with the likes of Oasis, Prince and the Rolling Stones performing.

City fans celebrate promotion on the pitch

Not everybody was happy with the events. This is groundsman Stan Gibson, who was somewhat dissatisfied with the amount of rigging left behind by the concert workers

Prince's 1992 *Diamonds and Pearls* tour at Maine Road

Noel Gallagher with Oasis in 1996

David Bowie performs at Maine Road, as part of his *Sound and Vision* tour in August 1990

62
FA YOUTH CUP FINAL
The future was Bright-well

Prior to the 2023 FA Cup final, the only national all-Manchester final played between City and United was the 1986 FA Youth Cup final. It was a two-legged encounter, with the first game ending 1-1 in front of an Old Trafford crowd of 7,602 (the City scorer was Paul Lake). The second leg was watched by 18,164 at Maine Road and ended in a 2-0 Blues win with David Boyd and Paul Moulden scoring. Steve Redmond was the captain who lifted the trophy.

63
IT WENT BANANAS
The yellow fruit craze

In the late 1980s, at a time when fan behaviour nationwide was under the spotlight, City supporters made headlines for all the right reasons. The fans started to take inflatable bananas to games and this led to the supporters of other clubs copying the idea. Frank Newton, a dedicated Blue, started the craze when he took a giant demonstration banana to the first home game of the 1987/88 season. He then began to take it to away games, including a match at Oldham played in heavy rain. Fans on the open away end were drenched, morale was low but the sight of this banana seemed to lift spirits and created a bit of humour on a miserable day.

By the end of that campaign, other inflatable bananas had appeared, while a chant for the City goalscorer Imre Varadi was adapted (the word banana replaced Varadi) to celebrate the presence of the bananas. The craze took off further in 1988/89 with away games, most notably at Stoke in December 1988, seeing thousands of inflatables. Bananas were regularly seen around Maine Road too as City's craze received praise from far and wide.

64
REMEMBER WHEN CITY SCORED 10?
The perfect score

The highest score ever at Maine Road was when City defeated Crystal Palace 11-4 in an FA Cup game in 1926. However, one of the most memorable high-scoring wins came in November 1987 when City defeated Huddersfield Town 10-1 in a Division Two match (pictured above, left and below). It was an incredible day but amazingly Huddersfield started the brighter team, putting City under real pressure for the opening minutes. A clinical strike from City's Neil McNab in the 12th minute changed things and from then on the Blues were dominant, with Paul Stewart, Tony Adcock and David White all scoring hat-tricks.

65
EDDIE LARGE
ON THE BENCH
The comedian

During the 1970s and 1980s the double act Little & Large were popular thanks to a Saturday night BBC TV show. Eddie Large was a well-known and much-loved City supporter who was a regular at games. Various City figures including Joe Royle, Kevin Keegan and physio Roy Bailey used to invite him behind the scenes, often as a morale-booster. He was allowed to sit alongside the substitutes and playing staff during games.

Look carefully at this photo (above right) and you might just spot him immediately to the left of the blue dugout, wearing a dark suit. It seems strange today allowing a prominent TV comedian on to the bench but this was one of those unusual things about City in those days.

66
PAUL LAKE
SWALLOWING
HIS TONGUE
The life-saver

City star Paul Lake is stretchered off after being knocked unconscious by a clash of heads with Leicester City's Paul Ramsey at Maine Road in March 1989. Only the quick actions of City trainer Roy Bailey saved Lake's life. Bailey hooked Lake's tongue out of his throat after he had swallowed it. The drama brought a strange atmosphere to the ground that day when the result seemed unimportant. For the record the Blues beat Leicester City 4-2.

67
THE 5-1
United who?

City 5-1 United. For many fans it was the best Manchester derby of the 1980s. Mel Machin's Blues thrashed Alex Ferguson's United team.

Andy Hinchcliffe celebrates with Ian Brightwell, Paul Lake and Ian Bishop in September 1989

68
THE FANZINE SELLERS
The fans had their say!

During the 1980s the fanzine movement started and City soon had a series of well-written and popular publications. The first was *Blue Print*, followed by *King of the Kippax*, *Electric Blue* and many others as seen by this image (above) of sellers in a tunnel at Maine Road. A corner of the forecourt outside the North Stand, close to the Kippax, became known as fanzine corner. For years fanzines were the only way fans could express their feelings on the game's issues. They gave Blues a voice. Two fanzines (Dave & Sue Wallace's *King of the Kippax* and an online version of Noel Bayley's *Bert Trautmann's Helmet*) still survive in 2023.

THE KIPPAX
The noise

Part of the Kippax captured during the 5-1 City win in the Manchester derby, in September 1989. The area seen here was where most of the noise came from. Chanting would typically be started by fans in 'The Sways' who would pack into the back section of the stand, close to the segregation fence.

70
WOMEN'S FOOTBALL
The Ladies' goal

Significant women's football games were played at Hyde Road (before the FA banned women's matches on FA affiliated grounds in 1921) and, of course, at the Etihad in recent seasons. The FA's ban was lifted by 1971 and in the years that followed the club's training facilities were used by the famous Manchester Corinthians team on occasion. In 1988 the club's own women's team was established. Originally known as Manchester City Ladies (and going strong today at the highest level as Manchester City Women) the club sometimes trained at Maine Road. It also played charity games at the stadium and sometimes exhibition games played before the men's league games.

Believe it or not this was part of Maine Road's first-team gym facilities under the Main Stand. Here members of the City Ladies team were photographed playing head tennis by Crosland Ward

Manchester City Ladies FC at Maine Road: photo by Crosland Ward in 1989

71
CLASSIC MAINE ROAD
The aerial view

This photograph of Maine Road in 1991 (below) shows what to many fans was 'classic Maine Road'. The North Stand is top with the Kippax on the right. The Platt Lane Stand is at the bottom of the photo.

72
QUINN IN NETS
The penalty save

City's meeting with Derby County in April 1991 was unusual as it saw striker Niall Quinn take over in goal. Blues goalkeeper Tony Coton was sent off before half-time for fouling Dean Saunders, conceding a penalty in the process. Quinn had already scored, and went on to save the Derby spot-kick. The 2-1 City win also relegated Derby.

73
PLATT LANE
The old stand

Looking towards the Platt Lane Stand on September 11, 1991. The main section of the old stand was built in 1935 and was demolished in 1992. For much of its existence it was a popular seated stand, though often uncomfortable. It consisted of wooden benches bolted on to the original terracing, but fans loved it.

74
SKY'S FIRST
Monday Night Football kicks off

Manchester City v QPR was scheduled for the first Sky Monday night live game on August 17, 1992. The match started with spectacle of cheerleaders (above) and ended in a 1-1 draw, with David White scoring the City goal.

Norman Wisdom entertaining the crowd at Maine Road

75
IS THAT PETER REID IN A FLAT CAP?
The Norman Wisdom visit

When City faced Oldham during the 1992/93 season supporters on the Kippax were somewhat surprised when they saw what they first thought to be player-manager Peter Reid enter the pitch wearing a flat cap. On closer inspection they soon discovered it was the veteran entertainer Norman Wisdom. During the following few minutes Norman did a full repertoire of tripping himself up and falling over while taking a penalty. It was a rather surreal scene to say the least.

76
PLAYER NAMED BARS
Thirsty work

Dotted all around Maine Road were bars named after former players. The Roy Clarke Bar was positioned in the new Platt Lane Stand from 1993 onwards while Malcolm's Bar was named after City's legendary coach Malcolm Allison and was one of the stadium's newest bars. It opened after the Main Stand re-fit of the mid-1990s. There were bars behind the old Kippax Stand, including one named after Denis Law, and in the recesses under both the North Stand and the Main Stand.

77
CITY v SPURS
The 5-2 win

An attendance of 25,473 (stadium capacity was reduced due to the Kippax being rebuilt) saw City beat an Ossie Ardiles Tottenham side 5-2 in 1994. The first half ended 3-1, with Paul Walsh (two) and Niall Quinn hitting the goals. Spurs made it 3-2 just after the break, but strikes from Steve Lomas and Garry Flitcroft completed the rout. It was a Maine Road classic.

Ossie Ardiles pondering how to be beat City on the day of the 5-2 defeat

78
THE BLUE PRINT FLAG
The giant banner

In the days before widespread large-scale flags, City fanzine *Blue Print* funded a flag which would be unveiled before games on the Kippax. It was huge and heavy, and it took fans hours to get it prepared and taken into the stadium on matchdays. City supporter Steve Worthington captured this image of it (above) on the Kippax at the stand's final day. By this time the flag had needed to be reduced in size due to tears and problems physically getting it into the stadium.

The Kippax's last stand v Chelsea - the *Blue Print* flag is seen from the Main Stand in April 1994

79
THE KIPPAX
The final game

Fans get ready for the Kippax's last stand at Maine Road in April 1994 (pictured left). The final game in front of the old terracing stand was a 2-2 draw with Chelsea. On its final day it was the largest standing terracing left in England.

80
THOSE HOUSES THAT OVERLOOKED THE GROUND
The free ticket

There was one corner of Maine Road that allowed a view into the stadium for people living around the ground. This gap at the corner, between the Kippax and Platt Lane Stand, allowed a few residents on neighbouring Thornton Road to watch games from their bedrooms. A couple of the houses decided to have loft conversions and on matchday there were often faces watching the action from the windows.

View from the other side of the wall

One of the houses during the City v Feyenoord friendly in August 1994

Controlled
ZONE

**1st Aug-31st May
1st Team Match Day**

Sat & Bank holiday
Noon-5·30pm

Sunday
1·00-6·30pm

Mon-Fri
5·30-10·30pm

KEEBUILDERS
061 477 6262

82
THE NEW KIPPAX
The new blue seats

Following the demolition of the old Kippax, a new all-seater stand holding over 10,000 was built. It became known as the new Kippax and was opened by Bert Trautmann in 1995. At times during its construction the capacity of Maine Road dropped to less than 20,000 – the lowest capacity the club had experienced since the 1890s.

Scott Hiley and Michael Brown shield the ball from Newcastle's Faustino Asprilla in 1996

83
CITY v NEWCASTLE
The '96 relegation

Although the late 1990s is often remembered as a time of struggle for City, the decade had started positively with the Blues hoping to challenge for the game's top honours. There were two fifth-place finishes in 1991 and 1992 amid a great deal of optimism. Things took a turn for the worse during the 1995/96 season when the Blues were relegated out of the Premier League for the first time but even then there were some memorable games. On February 24, 1996, a dramatic 3-3 draw against league leaders Newcastle had brought some hope that relegation could be avoided.

83
KINKLADZE GOAL
v SOUTHAMPTON
The special Georgian

Georgi Kinkladze was one of the most talented players to grace Maine Road in its final decade. Here he is (below) in June 1996 with chairman Francis Lee at a publicity shoot for the latest sponsorship deal with electronics firm Brother. The previous March the Georgian scored a goal which encapsulated his mesmerising talent. He picked up the ball on the right and danced his way through several challenges before dinking it over Southampton goalkeeper Dave Beasant. That day Kinkladze scored twice as the Blues won 2-1.

Noel (top) and Liam Gallagher on the pitch as City take on Portsmouth in 1997

85
OASIS
The 'Supersonic' boys

Prior to City's game with Portsmouth in August 1997, Oasis were brought on to the pitch to receive the acclaim of fans. The event became a little more newsworthy than anticipated when Liam Gallagher headed towards the away section and appeared to goad the Portsmouth fans. The game ended 2-2.

Watching from a box is Liam alongside actor Kevin Kennedy

This photo was taken by club photographer Ed Garvey from the 'Alan Ball' with the 'Gene Kelly' visible beyond the Kippax Stand (right)

86
THE GENE KELLY
'Singing in the Rain'

From the mid-1990s, after the Kippax Stand was built, the capacity of Maine Road was far too small to accommodate the numbers that wanted to attend games and so the club installed a series of temporary stands. The first was positioned in the corner between the North Stand and New Kippax. It became known as the 'Gene Kelly' as fans became used to 'singing in the rain'. That stand itself was later enlarged but others appeared in the corner between the Kippax and Platt Lane (that was dubbed the Alan Ball by a fanzine as it was 'small and didn't make much noise'), in the Platt Lane tunnel and behind the security room at the edge of the Main Stand and North Stand.

87
ABANDONED v IPSWICH
Rain stops play

Coincidentally, the last two abandoned games at Maine Road were both against Ipswich Town. These were the January 1994 league meeting which was 2-0 at the time it was stopped in the 39th minute and the December 2000 League Cup tie, which was 1-1 when it was abandoned after 23 minutes – both times due to torrential rain. City lost the replayed cup game in extra-time 2-1, with an attendance of 31,252.

In total eight City games were abandoned at Maine Road:
Brentford · November 1936
Blackpool · January 1956, FA Cup
Birmingham City · February 1958
Manchester United · August 1960
Norwich City · September 1965
Newcastle · February 1969
Ipswich · January 1994 and December 2000, League Cup

These programme pages are from the replayed game with Ipswich in 2000/01 season

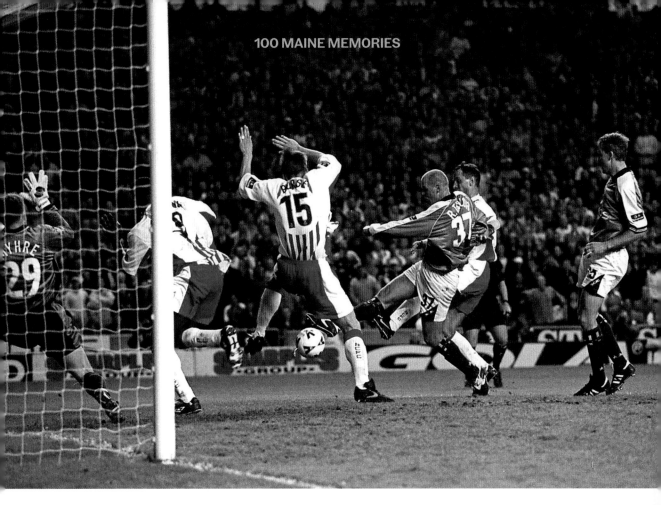

88
CITY v BIRMINGHAM
The Royle return

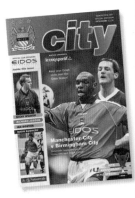

On April 28, 2000, Joe Royle's City went into the game against Birmingham City needing a win to gain promotion to the Premier League. The Blues got a 1-0 victory with Robert Taylor scoring the vital goal in the 40th minute (above). At the end of the game, the Maine Road pitch was invaded by fans in jubilant celebration.

Team celebrations for Taylor's winning goal

United's Fabien Barthez can only watch as City congratulate Shaun Goater on scoring the Blues' second goal

89
REMEMBER, REMEMBER THE 9TH NOVEMBER
The last derby at Maine Road

Looking from the new Kippax towards the Main Stand at the last Manchester derby to be played at Maine Road. The game ended 3-1 to City on November 9, 2002, with goals from Nicolas Anelka and Shaun Goater (two).

91
STUART PEARCE'S FINAL GAME
The skipper's last penalty

On the last day of the 2001/02 promotion season City defeated Portsmouth 3-1 with goals from Steve Howey, Shaun Goater and Jon Macken. But for many, the day belonged to captain Stuart Pearce.

It was revealed that Pearce was on 99 career goals and was desperate to reach his century in this, his final match. From the start, his every touch of the ball was met with the rousing cry of 'shoot' from the stands. It didn't seem to matter where he was, or how much of a chance he actually had.

As the game entered its final minute a miracle happened: City were awarded a penalty. Inevitably, Pearce was to take it. Another veteran, Dave Beasant, was in the Portsmouth goal and dropped a hint to Pearce he wouldn't move, but high drama followed as the City captain blasted the ball into the Platt Lane Stand. Nobody could believe his desperate luck. A goal then would not only have given Pearce his 100th goal but would also have taken City to 109 league goals – a new season record.

The agony was clearly etched on his face but within seconds he was laughing about his misfortune: "There is always a sting in the tail when Stuart Pearce does anything, and that penalty was comical. I have been psyched out by Dave Beasant!" he said. "The way I missed the goal just about sums me up, but it has been a pleasure and honour to represent the clubs I have, and I am very proud to have won this championship."

90
ROSE WOOLRICH'S ROOM
The legendary press room lady

Hidden away in the bowels of the Main Stand, off the tunnel closest to the Platt Lane Stand, was a tea room for photographers. This was Rose Woolrich's room. She had been making sandwiches and tea for the photographers throughout Maine Road's final 30 years or so. Rose made it a special part of the old ground and she always ensured the photographers were well looked after. Frequently Kevin Keegan, chairman John Wardle and other club officials would pop in to see Rose and grab a sneaky scone when she'd let them.

During Maine Road's final season club photographer Ed Garvey, a regular in the room himself, snapped these photos of the old place

WE ARE THE NORTH STAND
Singing the Blues

Once the Kippax – the final area of terracing – was demolished in 1994, the North Stand became the singing heartbeat of the club. Here it is during the last season at Maine Road, 2002/03.

mcfc.co.uk/juniorblues lecoqsportif lecoqsportif

93
BERNARD'S HONOUR
The final lock-up

Bernard Halford had been the club secretary for 30 years when Maine Road staged its final game in 2003. Afterwards he was given the honour of officially locking the gates for the last time.

Bernard Halford on his emotional return to the ground with Gary James during demolition in 2004

94
ELVIS – KIPPAX BIRD
The pigeon-scarer

Pigeons and other birds had often been a problem at Maine Road. Some nested in the old Kippax Stand and attempted to do the same when the new stand took its place in 1995. City's groundstaff decided to tackle this by hanging a plastic bird, designed to look like a bird of prey, in the new stand. When first spotted by fans who were mystified as to where he'd come from, he was dubbed Elvis. For the ground's final years Elvis became a 'must-see' sight on stadium tours and by fans sat in either the Kippax or the neighbouring 'Gene Kelly' temporary stand.

95
FOWLER
The last debut

Robbie Fowler was the last City player to make his debut at Maine Road – against West Brom in February 2003.

Here is Fowler during his debut (above), battling for the ball with Adam Chambers. Right: Fowler's name in lights as the Platt Lane scoreboard runs through the teams before kick-off

96
FOE TRIBUTES
The tragedy

The final days of Maine Road saw an outpouring of grief, with tributes laid for Marc Vivien Foe around the stadium. Foe had died of a heart-related condition after collapsing during Cameroon's 2003 FIFA Confederations Cup semi-final against Colombia.

Pictures by Gary James, showing tributes at Maine Road on June 30, 2003. City goalkeeper Carlo Nash (pictured in beige, carrying flowers) prepares to leave his personal tribute

97
FOE'S LEGACY
The last Maine Road goal

Marc Vivien Foe had scored the last City goal at Maine Road, coming in the 3-0 victory over Sunderland on April 21, 2003. That day he netted two with Robbie Fowler scoring the other before a sell-out crowd of 34,357.

Ed Garvey's image of Foe scoring against Sunderland in April 2003

Another of Ed Garvey's images shows Foe's rather subdued celebration that day (left)

Eddie Yates (left, a land drainage contractor), and Stan Gibson, the head groundsman at City, look at the plan before they begin to remove all the turf and topsoil from the pitch at Maine Road in October 1961

98
THAT EXTERNAL WALL!
Brick by brick...

The external wall of the ground used to wrap itself around the ground from either side of the Main Stand. Once the North Stand opened in the early 1970s the external wall was demolished behind that stand to provide a greater flow for spectators. The same happened in 1993 when the new Platt Lane Stand opened and this left only the external wall behind the Kippax. Even when a new Kippax Stand rose up in 1994/95 the club decided to retain the original external wall, with its turnstiles. It remained one of the few areas of the ground that those attending the stadium's first game in 1923 would recognise, although its height had altered over the years.

99
THE STAFF
The people inside City

Compared to the modern era there were few staff who worked at Maine Road each day. Most of them would rarely be seen by fans but between games the maintenance staff would be repairing seats, fences, cleaning the stadium and much more.

Current groundsman Lee Jackson at work during the League Cup tie with Ipswich at Maine Road in 2000

100
THE PLAYERS
The Maine Road greats

A selection of the teams who have played on the hallowed turf of Maine Road and have brought joy and entertainment to the thousands of fans who have come through the gates of Maine Road.

MANCHESTER CITY F.C.

The 1936 City team pose next to the Main Stand. Notice the church in the distance. That was St Matthews and was replaced by the City Social Club in 1966

City in 1947/48 with the Scoreboard End (later North Stand) behind. Back row (left to right): Joe Fagan, Bert Sproston, Frank Swift, Eric Westwood, Albert Emptage. Front: Jackie Wharton, Andy Black, Les McDowall, Eddie McMorran, George Smith, Roy Clarke

Team photo from 1976/77 in front of the Kippax: Back row (left to right): Dave Watson, Joe Royle, Keith MacRae, Joe Corrigan, Tommy Booth, Tony Henry
Middle row: Roy Bailey (trainer), Peter Barnes, Glyn Pardoe, Kenny Clements, Paul Power, Mick Docherty, Mike Lester, Willie Donachie, Gary Owen, Ken Barnes (trainer)
Front: Tony Book (manager), Ged Keegan, Jimmy Conway, Brian Kidd, Mike Doyle, Asa Hartford, Colin Bell, Dennis Tueart , Bill Taylor (coach)

A
LONG
GOODBYE
TO
MAINE ROAD

Manchester City F.C.

End
of an
Era

For our last season at Maine Road, 2002/2003, photographer and lifelong fan **Kevin Cummins** was given the dream job – an access-all-areas pass to capture every last moment of history before we said a final farewell to the place we had called home for so long. He looks back on that season and digs out some amazing images

MCFC

MAINE ROAD

1923 -

2003

We're not really here

Manchester City's final season at Maine Road

Kevin Cummins

CITY

This season is the 20th anniversary of our move from Maine Road. As many of you already know, I spent the whole of 2002/03 producing a book for the football club. The book *We're not Really Here* is my loving tribute to the longest running saga in my life: Manchester City FC.

When I approached the club, I thought it'd be more difficult to convince them of my idea. Football clubs are notorious closed shops at times. I was also worried that if I got too close to the club, we'd ultimately fall out, and my love affair with the Blues would be over. Nothing like that happened. I felt even closer to them as we approached the finishing line. Everyone at the club was an absolute delight to work with.

The manager at the time, a certain Kevin Keegan, told me I could come and go as I pleased. He'd never tell me to get out of his face. He said, "If I'm giving them a rollocking on a Monday, stand next to me and capture the look on their faces." He told me the only things he didn't want me to do were to go in the dressing room after a game and to travel on the team bus.

I told him I wouldn't need anything like that anyway. The book was essentially about the area, the stadium, the fans, and the players, who spent that final season representing this great historic club of ours.

The fans were great. Many knew me of course, and the ones who didn't, soon got to know me. Many suggested people I should photograph. Several others would look after my camera gear when I'd leave bits of it on the perimeter wall as I'd chase off after another photo opportunity.

Our first game at home that season was Newcastle United. I was sat by the goalpost at the Platt Lane End, when Huckerby scored the only goal to give us three points on our return to the Premier League. I forgot I was chronicling the season when he scored, and I dropped my camera when I punched the air and almost ran on the pitch to celebrate with Darren. Fortunately, I just stopped myself in time, or it would have been the shortest book in existence. I realised I had to be more professional, but there were other moments when I was so wrapped up with what I was doing, I'd forget that I had almost 40,000 pairs of eyes watching me, or more accurately, waiting for me to get off the pitch so as the game could start.

When I started shooting photos for the book, although I had a few ideas mapped out, it didn't always go according to plan. I like the idea of repetitive patterns on pages. I decided I'd shoot the teams running out on the pitch together for each game, more or less from the same spot, and we'd then run 18 across a double page spread, with the 19th – our final game (v Southampton) on a full page. This worked really well.

I also thought we'd do similar with a photo each week of the away fans. The first game v Newcastle was fine. The Toon Army were good humoured and many fans were chatting to me and asking what I was shooting for. The next game, v Everton, was awful. Their fans were belligerent, at best, and were throwing coins and plastic bottles at me. One threatened me, then called the police over to say I'd sworn at him. I decided to scrap this idea. I wanted to enjoy the project, not put myself in danger each week.

I decided it'd be safer, and more fun, to photograph our fans in the corner of the Kippax, 'bantering' with the away supporters. I occasionally photographed a few opposition fans. The Liverpool fan with the *Financial Times* was a favourite, and kind of summed up the direction modern Premier League football was heading in.

FANS

It was an absolute thrill for me to be able to work with City's Former Players Association when I was putting the book together. Originally, I thought I'd be able to ask for a handful of players, but they were able to get different generations of former City greats together for me to photograph. It was important to have them represented in the book, after all, they were a huge part of the story and history of the stadium.

When I photographed Mike Summerbee, I asked him to look out across the pitch and to conjure up memories of time past. When I told him I'd finished the session, he didn't move. I touched his shoulder and he apologised, and said, "I was imagining that I was just getting on the end of a lovely ball from Colin Bell, for our fifth goal against United." I said that was quite a dream. To which he replied, "It was only the end of the first half."

Towards the end of the season, I thought it'd make a good shot to get Eyal Berkovic with Colin Bell, as Eyal played a similar role in that season's side. Colin was reluctant, but he often was when it came to having his photo taken.

"You think he plays in a similar position to the one I played?" he asked me. "Well, kind of," I replied. "Aye, right. How long have you been watching football for, Kevin?" he responded.

I laughed, nervously. Fair play to Colin though, he did the photo as I requested, but, if ever a picture told a story, this is it.

One of the things I wanted to capture was the complete chaos of the signage at Maine Road. If you look around the Etihad, you'll notice there's a proper identity and uniformity to signage and branding. This wasn't the case at Maine Road. Signage was from different generations, and nobody seemed to think old signs should be replaced or updated. Of course, this gave it a certain charm, but this was 2003, not 1923.

I know many of you still wish we were at Maine Road. I understand it's where a lot of us older fans started watching football when we were kids, but let's face it, it wasn't the greatest place to watch football. It was comfortable, familiar, a home from home if you like, but there were some precarious positions and obstructed views in many parts of the stadium.

Most City fans were aware of the project I was working on and were (generally) delighted to be asked to pose for a portrait outside and around the stadium. I wanted to use all the elements around the ground: the brickwork, the shuttered shop windows *et al*, to give the photos some urban context.

The guy holding the mobile phone – with the City badge on screen – is another photo that locates the photo perfectly in time. I was toying with the idea of doing a short interview with each person, about their favourite memory of Maine Road, or similar, but it was too time-consuming. I only really had time to take their photo. I did ask the guy with the red and black '69 kit if he was sorry to be leaving Maine Road for pastures new and he replied: "Not really. It's never been the same since they put a roof on the Scoreboard End. That was the beginning of the end for me." It's worth noting that the roof went on the 'scoreboard end' 30 years earlier. A true traditionalist if ever there was one.

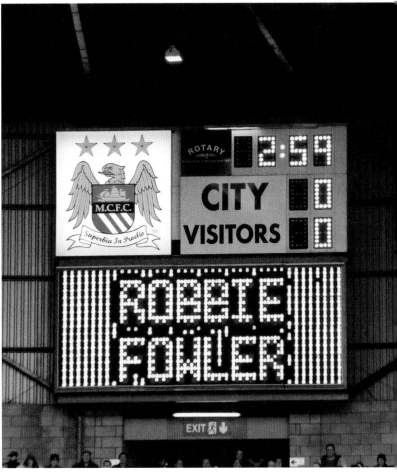

When we were planning the editorial flow of the book, we decided to feature two matches: Versus Manchester United and Arsenal. All games were covered of course, but these two would have at least one spread of photos each. Nicolas Anelka playing against his old club was of interest, of course, but I also wanted to watch Kevin Keegan and his reactions during the game.

When I arrived on matchday, acting chairman John Wardle was hanging around outside the Arsenal dressing room door, waiting to get Thierry Henry to sign an Arsenal shirt. When Henry ran out to warm up, loads of City fans were trying to get an autograph. Henry was an absolute superstar who everyone wanted to see.

Prior to kick-off, I was on the pitch photographing Nico chatting to his former teammates: Vieira, Henry and Pires, when I heard someone shout, "Oi! Will you get off the pitch so I can start the game!" I looked round, and it was referee Paul Durkin, laughing and gesturing at me to get off the pitch. I'd completely lost track of time, and place, I was so immersed in getting the photos. I meekly trotted off, tempted to give it the time-wasting round of applause to all four sides of the ground, but one more look from Durkin made me think better of it.

Arsenal – especially Henry, were astonishing that day. Even many City fans applauded them off at the end of the game. I 'can't remember' the score that day, but I know Anelka scored against his old side. I think we've more than made up for the lesson we were given that day over the past few seasons. Long may it continue.

Another editorial decision I made early on was wanting to photograph a band around the stadium. I thought it'd tie in well with my 'other job' of photographing musicians. I also felt it would work well with City's strong links with bands around the city, who were mainly Blues.

I'd photographed Oasis at Maine Road twice, and not wanting to repeat myself, I thought it'd be good to photograph a more emerging band. This way it'd connect well with the 'end of an era; start of a new era' theme that I was aiming to propagate.

I contacted Doves, and they were delighted to do it with me. It wasn't an easy shoot, as I wanted the stadium to be a part of the shoot too; not just the band. But once I realised it was part of it anyway, and it didn't have to be the most prominent feature, I was able to shoot in my normal style. I then agonised for ages as to whether or not the photos should be in black and white or colour – so I shot both.

Mark Farrow, the designer, decided on colour as he felt black and white wouldn't work in the book, with every other photo being in highly saturated colour.

DOVES

Southampton was the final game at Maine Road. It was a very emotional day for everyone; fans, players, staff, at Manchester City.

Kevin Keegan finally invited me into the dressing room pre-match, as he was making Shaun Goater captain in his final game for the club. I took a lovely photo of regular skipper Sylvain Distin putting the armband on Goater.

Lots of former players were invited, and lots of old faces – fans as well – turned up for this special day. In typical City fashion, we contrived to lose the match 0-1, but that didn't seem to matter. The day was somehow bigger than the game.

The club arranged a post-match concert on the pitch, but most people seemed to want to sit in silence remembering some of the great occasions we'd all been witness to. The Ballet on Ice in '67/68; Colin's comeback against Newcastle; the 5-2 drubbing of Tottenham; Schalke 04 in the Cup Winners' Cup semi-final, the many times we'd hammered our local rivals, and so on.

We all had our favourite moments at Maine Road, and this was the end of an era. In August we'd all be changing our routines of many years. What did the future hold for us? Could we finally dream of winning a trophy again?

WE'RE BACK

'THEY'RE NOT REALLY HERE'

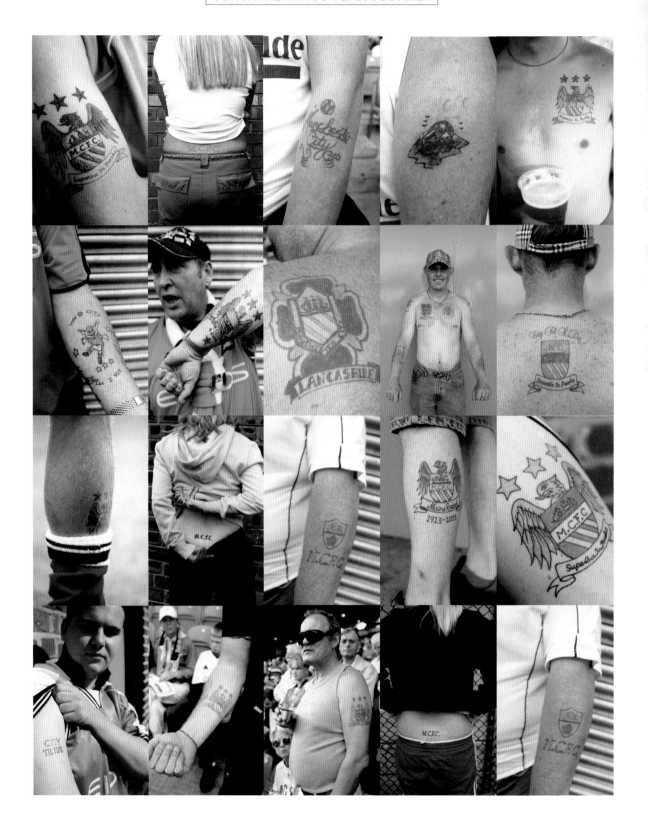

BLUE MOON

KEEGAN

1923-2003

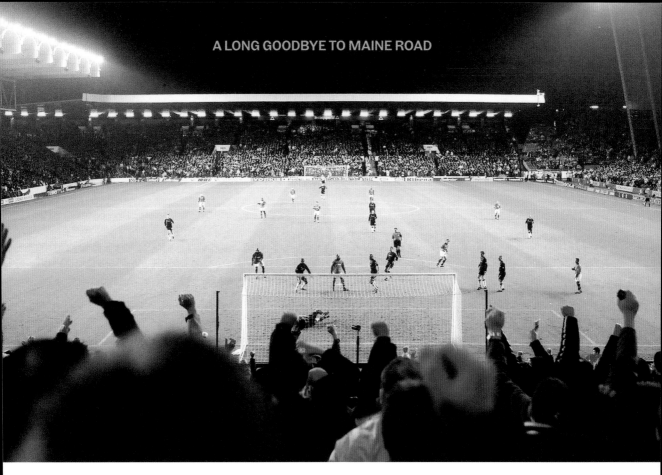

A LONG GOODBYE

START OF A DREAM

20 YEARS OF THE ETIHAD

Goals, glory, trophies and celebrations – our first two decades in the stadium have been a fantastic ride. We round up the most memorable (and some of the funniest) moments so far...

No.1 ★ FIRSTS

★ FIRST NAME
It was named the City of Manchester Stadium – or CoMS for short – by the city council before construction even began, though to many it was also known as Eastlands, or even Sport City, as the general area around the ground was called. Our home officially became the Etihad Stadium in July 2011.

★ FIRST COMPETITIVE GAME
There had been a friendly win over Barcelona, with Nicolas Anelka grabbing the winner, but the first competitive match came against Welsh side TNS in the UEFA Cup on August 14, 2003. Trevor Sinclair scored the first competitive goal at the stadium after 14 minutes of the 5-0 win.

★ FIRST PREMIER LEAGUE GOAL
Portsmouth were the visitors for the first league game and their striker Yakubu was the scorer of the first Premier League goal, after 24 minutes, before City defender David Sommeil equalised in the last minute – the first of many such goals here over the next 20 years!

★ FIRST EFL CUP SEMI-FINAL
City have been regulars in EFL Cup semi-finals with a total of eight appearances over the 20 Etihad years. Only seven have actually taken place at this stadium – the usually two-legged tie became a single game one year due to Covid in 2021. But the very first of the seven took place in January 2010 and saw City beat Manchester United 2-1.

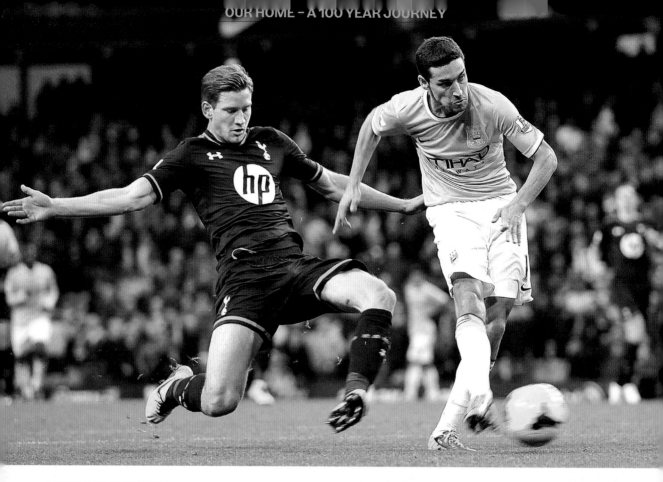

★ FIRST AND FASTEST ▲
The first goal of the 6-0 win over Spurs in November 2013 was scored by Jesus Navas after 13 seconds! Still the fastest goal at the Etihad.

★ FIRST 'HAWK-EYE' GOAL
City's 100th goal of the 2013/14 season was scored by Edin Dzeko in a 4-2 win over Cardiff in January but it was memorable for also being the first goal ever awarded by the Premier League's new goal-line technology system. City would go on to net 100 times in the league, the first time we had done so since 1957/58.

★ FIRST CHAMPIONS LEAGUE GAME ▶
This arrived on September 14, 2011 when an Aleksandar Kolarov second-half equaliser earned a point against Napoli after Edinson Cavani had given them the lead.

★ FIRST CHAMPIONS LEAGUE SEMI-FINAL
Manuel Pellegrini achieved that target in April 2016 when City hosted Real Madrid in a goalless first leg draw before going out in a heartbreaking 1-0 loss a week later.

★ FIRST PREMIER LEAGUE TITLE
The 2011/12 season famously ended with the Etihad crowning City champions for the first time ... but there were plenty of other firsts along the way. City were unbeaten at home and became the first Premier League team to win 20 consecutive home games, dating back to the previous season.

⋆ FIRST CHAMPIONS LEAGUE SEMI-FINAL WIN ▲
Fast forward to May 2021 and an unstoppable Riyad Mahrez was on the mark twice in a 2-0 win over PSG, adding to the goal he had scored in the 2-1 first-leg victory a week earlier. The result carried City through to a first-ever Champions League final.

⋆ FIRST TO 150 ...
City's second league title, in 2013/14, also saw us become the first team to ever score 150 goals (in all competitions) in a single season. The Blues would end with 156, beating the previous record of 143, set by Manchester United in 1956/57.

⋆ AND FIRST TO 100 ...
Premier League title number three, in 2017/18, saw City become the first team to bag 100 points in a season. The team earned the nickname 'The Centurions' in the process.

⋆ FIRST TO 100, AGAIN ...
In January 2019, City became the first club across Europe's main leagues to hit 100 in all competitions in that season – not surprising given that the Blues had just won home cup games 7-0 and 9-0, against Rotherham and Burton, respectively. Pep Guardiola's team went on to break their own record, ending the campaign with 169 goals, as they became the first team in history to win an English domestic treble of league, FA and League Cups.

⋆ FIRST TO 39 ▶
Erling Haaland's stunning five-goal performance in the 7-0 win over RB Leipzig in the Champions League set a new club record for the most goals in a season, surpassing Tommy Johnson's tally of 38 across the 1928/29 season.

⋆ 2020/21 ▲
Another title and yet more firsts, including the first top-flight team to win 21 consecutive games in all competition; most consecutive league wins from the start of a season for a top-flight team (13), while City also equalled our own club record by going 28 games unbeaten in all competitions.

No.2 ✶ DERBY DELIGHT

Shaun Wright-Phillips' wonder goal ... hat-tricks for Phil Foden and Erling Haaland ... a Vincent Kompany header effectively winning the Premier League ... clashes with a Wembley place at stake.

Manchester derbies have always been guaranteed to be one of the highlights of every season but in the Etihad era, they have taken on even more significance.

That was certainly the case in April 2012, in the penultimate home game of the season, when the Reds visited in the closing stages of a thrilling title race between the Manchester clubs.

Although there would be drama to come, the derby that day was billed as a title decider so when inspirational skipper Vincent Kompany rose just before half-time to head in David Silva's corner for the game's only goal, the Etihad exploded.

Just three weeks after we had trailed United by eight points, City were now top on goal difference and just needed to win our last two games to clinch our first-ever Premier League title.

Two weeks later, we did just that, of course, with Sergio Aguero's injury-time winner against QPR, but without Kompany's heroics, who knows if the Argentine's iconic moment would've happened.

A couple of seasons later, with Manuel Pellegrini now in charge, came another unforgettable derby day – for the blue half of Manchester, at least – when City's 4-1 win seemed to herald a new era under the new manager.

Sergio Aguero scored twice, including a lethal volley, but Samir Nasri was City's man of the match and scored a superb volley himself to complete the rout.

There was another big derby win, on the way to another title, in March 2022 when Kevin De Bruyne and Riyad Mahrez each scored twice, for one of three home derbies that have ended in a 4-1 City win during the Etihad years.

And the following season saw another unforgettable occasion, and the highest-scoring Manchester derby ever, when City ran out 6-3 winners in an extraordinary clash.

Foden and Haaland could each lay claim to the match ball after scoring hat-tricks – the first time in Etihad history two players have scored trebles in the same match – and the Blues actually led by a thumping 6-1 scoreline until United pulled two goals back in the last six minutes.

Then there have been lower scoring games with, arguably, even higher stakes – specifically, a place in the EFL Cup final at Wembley.

League Cup semi-finals are, of course, usually two-legged affairs which mean supporters have been left with confusing feelings on last-four derby days.

In January 2010, Carlos Tevez scored twice in a 2-1 win ... only for City to lose the return leg and miss out on Wembley.

And 10 years later, the roles were reversed as United won 1-0 but City fans could still celebrate, as the 3-1 first leg victory at Old Trafford ensured they advanced to the final where they lifted the trophy in a 2-1 win over Aston Villa.

But ask any City fan of a certain age for their favourite derby memory and it may well prove to be the first ever at the Etihad, in March 2004.

United were still very much the more successful team in the city back in those early days, so hosting the first-ever derby at the Etihad gave fans hope of a change in fortune. How those hopes were answered!

Robbie Fowler started the rout, Jon Macken volleyed in a second, Trevor Sinclair got in on the act and Wright-Phillips wrapped up the 4-1 win with a brilliant drive.

"The derby was a massive one," recalls City striker Macken. "It was the first one in the new stadium and to win 4-1 was a great achievement.

"I remember the ball hitting the back of the net; that's about it! I swivelled onto it and then, after that, I was off, running away to celebrate. I've seen a few pictures, obviously, and I think there is quite an iconic one of a very young Cristiano Ronaldo standing in the background with his hands on his hips.

"Man United were, and are, such a talented squad and an unbelievable club so to get a result like that, in that manner, made it so memorable and fills you with pride, still to this day. Fans seem to remember it and that makes me proud too."

No.3 ★ TITLE # 1

If there is one soundtrack, one word even, that will live forever in Manchester City and Etihad folklore, it was uttered on May 13, 2012. And if there is one set of numbers that do the same, then "93.20" arrived on this afternoon as well.

It was the day many City fans had been waiting for their whole lives, and one that was all the sweeter because of the intense, heart-stopping drama that accompanied it.

By the time the dust had settled, after 93 minutes and 20 seconds against QPR, Sergio Aguero had sealed a 3-2 win that clinched the Premier League crown and veteran TV commentator Martin Tyler had provided the refrain that launched thousands of City ringtones for years to come.

And, for the first time in history, a City captain had a Premier League trophy in his possession.

It is hard to remember now, after events of that day over a decade ago, that the previous home game, a 1-0 win over their closest rivals in the table, Manchester United, had been every bit as nerve-jangling as this final-day chaos.

After trailing United by eight points, with six games left, that derby victory took City above them into first place and meant that victories in their last two games guaranteed the Blues the title. A trip to Newcastle was nervy but two goals in the last 20 minutes from Yaya Toure saw City home 2-0 and, with relegation-threatened QPR visitors to the Etihad on the final day, many fans might have thought the hard work was done.

Former City boss Mark Hughes was in charge of Rangers, ex-Blues Shaun Wright-Phillips, Nedum Onuoha and Joey Barton were in their team and when Pablo Zabaleta fired the Blues into a first-half lead, the job looked as good as done.

But with the celebrations already starting around the Etihad, Djibril Cisse raced through to equalise and, with United leading their game at Sunderland, as the scores then stood, City had lost the league.

Barton was sent off a few minutes later, sparking a melee and some ugly scenes, before City conceded a second, to Jamie Mackie's header. A morale-destroying disaster loomed for the Blues.

Edin Dzeko's header on 92 minutes looked like nothing more than a cruel reminder of how close City had come as United's game finished in a victory up at Sunderland. The Reds were on course to become champions again.

But with City waiting 44 years for a league title, the football gods had other ideas.

Mario Balotelli and Aguero certainly hadn't given up, as the game clock read 93:20. The Italian provided the assist for his Argentinian team-mate and Aguero took a controlling touch before burying an unstoppable shot past QPR keeper Paddy Kenny.

Grown men, women and children burst into tears: Aguero ripped off his shirt; keeper Joe Hart ran screaming around the penalty area and manager Roberto Mancini and his staff seemed to out-celebrate everyone.

And, of course, Tyler summed it up with one word that has gone down in City – make that, English football – history. "Aguerooooooo!!!!"

"It is the best memory that I will ever have in my head," said the Argentinian striker when discussing the moment, before his last game for the club nine years later.

"I don't think it will happen again in another country or in this one. It's not something that can be repeated."

It was a day which everyone involved, as participant or observer, will never forget. Gareth Barry had started the game but was substituted for goalscorer Dzeko in the second half.

"Roberto was a really superstitious guy and once something had happened and worked he always stuck to it," explains Barry over a decade later.

"Edin had come on a couple of times for me and scored goals so he went to that plan. I don't know if it was plan B, C, or D! I was fearing the worst at that moment but anything can happen in football.

"We had a squad of great characters, the rapport between the lads was fantastic. It was an amazing time, and amazing feeling."

Even the losers that day could remember it fondly as results elsewhere meant QPR stayed up. For Onuoha, especially, it was a bittersweet loss.

"I just remember the high stakes of it all because City were going for the title and we were trying to stay up," he says.

"We were under pressure, and as things stood at half-time, we were going down. But the second half was one of the wildest halves of football I've ever seen.

"We took the lead, went down to 10 men, but City just seemed so far out of it. Their worst 15 minutes of the season were the 15 minutes before they scored their second. They were running out of ideas, the crowd was getting frustrated – the fans just seemed resigned that this was 'typical City'. City were going to lose the title, United were going to win it.

"But in a way, I think that was the end of the 'old City' and the beginning of the new one. When you play, you can't be a 'fan boy' so all I cared about was us staying up. But still, it was nice to be able to go to friends like Joe Hart and Micah (Richards) and congratulate them for winning the title."

And, of course, it was a goal and a title win heard around the world. Hundreds of miles away, in a corner of Spain, a young, aspiring footballer was watching the moment and drawing his own inspiration from it.

"I remember. I was a child and I remember following it," said current City midfielder Rodrigo.

"It was unbelievable. At the time, United used to be the team who won the leagues and with this goal, Sergio won the first title of this new era. It was crazy, unbelievable and I have good memories of this moment."

So, too, does every City supporter.

No.4 ∗ SERGIO

It began with two goals on his debut against Swansea in August 2011 and ended, predictably, with two more in an emotional farewell win against Everton 10 years later.

In between, Sergio Aguero's love affair with the Etihad seemed to know no bounds as he wrote his name into Manchester City folklore.

And no story of the Etihad, of course, would be complete without recounting the incredible events of May 13, 2012; a date that will live forever in the club's history.

The story of that goal is told elsewhere, and even if that Premier League title-winning goal against QPR had been the only one Aguero ever scored in his Etihad career, it would be sufficient to grant him City immortality.

But that was just one of 260 goals that the Argentina international, signed for £38 million from Atletico Madrid in July 2011, scored for the Blues.

And from the moment he made his first appearance for the club a month later, it was obvious Aguero had a special talent.

That day against Swansea, he came off the bench for his debut after 60 minutes and had the first of those 260 goals just eight minutes later, tapping in a Micah Richards cross, before adding a spectacular 30-yard drive in the dying seconds – the first but definitely not the last dramatic late Aguero goal that the Etihad would witness.

If everyone agrees the title-winner was their favourite Aguero goal at the Etihad, then there is a long list to choose from when City fans discuss their other favourite Kun moments.

The day he scored five goals in 20 thrilling minutes, either side of half-time, in a 6-1 win over Newcastle in October 2015 would be high on that list.

So, too, would be the hat-trick he plundered against mighty Bayern Munich when City beat the Germans 3-2 a year earlier, the first of his treble coming from a penalty he had won himself.

Just a month before that unforgettable evening, Aguero had scored all the City goals in a 4-1 win over Tottenham – with two coming from the spot – and February 2018 saw him hit another four, this time in a 5-1 victory against Leicester that set City up for a run that would deliver them the Premier League title.

As well as quantity, there was quality as well, of course. Whether it was the goal he scored from an almost impossible angle after a mistake in the Liverpool defence in the 2012/13 season, a thumping volley in the 4-1 derby win over United in the next campaign or the long-range strike in the 6-0 win over Chelsea in February 2019 – Aguero had an eye for the spectacular.

His goals were a key reason that Aguero was crowned a Premier League title winner five times in his 10 seasons with the club although by the time he collected the last of those, in 2020/21, he was hampered by injuries.

Still, a living legend like Aguero was not going to go quietly and, as City celebrated the lifting of another league title in the last home game of the season against Everton, he ended his Etihad career as he started it – as a goalscoring sub.

Put on after 65 minutes, Aguero hit the net twice in the next 11 minutes to clinch a 5-0 win, taking him on to 184 league goals in 275 games for City and breaking Wayne Rooney's record for the most Premier League goals for a single club into the bargain.

It was the last in a long list of hugely impressive achievements by one of the true greats of City history.

No.5 ★ TITLE #2

Two years after the craziest final day in City history, Manuel Pellegrini's men had another chance to be crowned Premier League champions.

It says everything about the 2012 title heroics, inspired by Sergio Aguero, that the 2014 success seems almost routine by comparison nearly 10 years later.

But in its own way, City's march to their second Premier League title was every bit as dramatic, and incredible, as the first had been.

Why? Because with two weeks of the season remaining, it looked as though Liverpool were going to end their wait for a first league title since 1990.

In a topsy-turvy campaign, the lead of the Premier League changed hands an amazing 25 times and City only held top spot for a grand total of 15 days throughout the whole season.

And with just three matches left, Liverpool manager Brendan Rodgers had a commanding five-point lead at the top of the table and the title was on its way to Anfield.

Not for the first time, however, the football fates had other ideas and City were gearing up for a momentous end to the campaign which saw them win their last five games in a 20-day spell.

And as City kept winning, Liverpool were stunningly beaten at home by Chelsea and held to a draw at Crystal Palace.

Now came the midweek game in hand for Pellegrini's side, a home one with Aston Villa at a rain-soaked Etihad, which the Blues had to win to regain top place. After a nervous, goalless first hour, Edin Dzeko popped up with the first of his two goals and City ran out 4-0 winners.

City were now top of the table by two points with just one game to play although, after what Etihad supporters had witnessed two years earlier, they could have been forgiven for thinking anything could happen on the final day.

Just two days short of the second anniversary of the Aguero title winner, City only needed a point against West Ham ... but still, as the game headed towards half-time, a City side that had already scored over 100 league goals could not find a way through.

That changed on 39 minutes when Samir Nasri scored a well-taken goal from 20 yards and City fans could relax. They certainly could after half-time, when captain Vincent Kompany turned in from close range after a Dzeko shot had been blocked, and the three points were in the bag – 2-0.

The title was City's by two points, and they ended the season with 102 league goals – at the time, the second-highest ever total – while they became the first-ever team to have three players all score more than 15 league goals: Aguero, Toure and Dzeko.

"The most important thing was we changed absolutely the way this team play," said Pellegrini. "I am not criticising other styles or comparing. I like to play one way, and, for me, it was very important to give the reasons and to have the trust of the players to change the way they played before.

"I think the way we played was as important as winning the title. We have players to play on the counter-attack but, for me, to win titles just in that way, I will not be happy. We won with 102 goals, and with the record of goals in all competitions in the history here in England. It is the way the team must play with the quality of players we have. It has been a brilliant season and I would say of all the sides we kept going the longest in all four competitions."

No.6 ✶ LET'S ALL DO THE POZNAN

From the fans who gave the football world inflatable bananas in the 1980s, it's no surprise that the Etihad years have brought some unforgettable, emotional and downright wacky moments in the stands.

✶THE POZNAN

There is only one place to start – and that is in the Europa League with the Polish side Lech Poznan, of course.

In October 2010, the Polish club came to the Etihad and City ran out 3-1 winners, with an Emmanuel Adebayor hat-trick that was quickly overshadowed by what happened among the visiting fans.

Midway through the game, Poznan fans turned their backs on the action, linked arms and bounced up and down in the distinctive dance that City supporters soon borrowed and, more than a decade later, still perform regularly.

*PYJAMA PARTY

In October 2005, City played Everton at the Etihad in a game which, because of bizarre TV timings, kicked off at 11.15am.

It was a game Danny Mills recalls, as he scored the first goal in a 2-0 win – his only one for the club – although the defender also remembers it for another reason.

As might be expected, City fans had a humorous response to the unsociable kick-off time.

"The goal wasn't bad! I think every year my goal gets a yard farther out," jokes Mills. "I think by now it's from my own six yard box!

"But it was that ridiculously early kick-off, 11:15 on a Sunday, and a lot of City fans turned up in pyjamas."

*TOURE TRIBUTE

Yaya and Kolo are two of the most popular and successful City stars of the last 20 years so, of course, loyal fans were going to pay tribute to the brothers.

In September 2012, before a game at Stoke, fans put together the first known "performance" of the Toure song, put to the tune of 1990s euro disco hit *No Limit*.

Within weeks, it had become a regular part of City fans' repertoire and, later that year, the brothers were filmed reacting with delight to the song after being shown footage of the tribute by the club's media department.

★ WE'RE NOT REALLY HERE

Okay, technically this chant dates back to the 1990s and became best known when the Blues were winning promotion from the third tier of English football under Joe Royle.

But as City have enjoyed far more success in the Etihad years, *We're Not Really Here* remains a staple of supporters' offerings on matchday.

The exact origins of the chant are unclear but it resonated back in the days when City were sailing in some unfamiliar waters. It's now a reminder of how far we have come as a club. "I never stopped smiling at the City fans. I still smile now when I'm watching telly or I'm at a game and the crowd goes up, singing *We're Not Really Here*, which was probably the best chant of all time," Royle told the club website.

"Gallows humour – I don't know where it started. Was it York, Port Vale or Wycombe? It was certainly in the outposts of football, and whenever I see City fans, they tell me they loved that season – that they really enjoyed it."

No.7 ★ CAPTAINS

From Sylvain Distin to Ilkay Gundogan, with six City favourites in between, there have been eight official club captains to lead out the Blues in the Etihad era.

There have been plenty of occasional skippers who have worn the armband on a temporary basis in the two decades at this stadium, of course.

But when it comes to the 'official' role, there have been just eight to hold that prestigious title – and all of them had moments to remember.

Certainly that is true in the case of Gundogan, whose two goals as a substitute in the final game of the 2021/22 season clinched a dramatic come-from-behind victory against Aston Villa and helped City hold onto the Premier League title.

Technically, Gundogan was not captain that day, with veteran midfielder Fernandinho skippering the Blues in his final game before bringing down the curtain on a brilliant career with the club.

Fernandinho had worn the armband for two years, taking over from another City legend, David Silva, who had held the position for the 2019/20 campaign – three seasons between them in which City won the league twice.

But when it comes to City captains, the conversation tends to come back to one man ... Vincent Kompany.

Signed from German club Hamburger SV in 2008, the classy defender was part of the City side that ended their 35-year wait for honours by winning the 2011 FA Cup final against Stoke.

Carlos Tevez was City skipper at Wembley that day, and the first to get his hands on a trophy since the Blues won the 1976 League Cup final, at the end of his one season as club captain.

But Kompany's leadership skills made him the obvious choice to take over in the summer of 2011, as the Belgian took hold of an armband he would keep until he left the club eight years later.

During those years, there were a steady stream of trophies passing through Kompany's hands and, while his inspirational leadership is never forgotten, the number of crucial goals the defender chipped in sometimes are.

In the spring of 2012, Kompany headed in a David Silva cross to win a crucial Manchester derby, three games from the end of the season. It was the only goal of the game and set up the final day drama when Sergio Aguero's winner secured the first of four Premier League titles Kompany would lift as captain.

Two years later, he was on the scoresheet again, as City beat West Ham 2-0 to win his second title, and in his final season, and in his last game at the Etihad, he thumped in a 70th-minute, 30-yard winner against Leicester which saw the Blues hold off Liverpool for another title. "We just wanted to hug him and kiss him and say thank you for that goal," recalls Bernardo Silva.

"There have been many important contributors to Manchester City's renaissance, but arguably none are more important than Vincent Kompany," Khaldoon Al Mubarak said in his tribute after the skipper's retirement.

"He defines the essence of the club. For a decade he has been the lifeblood, the soul, and beating heart of a supremely talented squad."

Kompany was continuing a proud tradition of City central defenders as captains, with the list of official club skippers during the Etihad era starting with Distin (2003-06), Richard Dunne (2006-09) and Kolo Toure (2010-11).

★ **... AND NOT FORGETTING ...**

Under Pep Guardiola, City have adopted a policy of players electing a number of vice-captains, meaning the armband has been passed around on occasion.

Kevin De Bruyne, the club's longest-serving player at the end of 2022/23, is one of the vice-captains ... and it's no surprise.

By the end of his eighth season at the Etihad, in the summer of 2023, the Belgium international had already helped City to five league titles, five EFL Cups, two FA Cups and victory in the 2023 Champions League final.

He was also twice named the Premier League Player of the Year and twice voted the Players' Player of the Year by the PFA.

Little wonder he is already considered one of our all-time legends ... while still a player at the Etihad.

No.8 * CULT HEROES

A set of loyal supporters like City's always adopt their favourite stars and they quickly become cult heroes. Many are featured elsewhere but, here, we look at just a few more crowd favourites from the Etihad years...

★ MARIO BALOTELLI ◄

There was never any doubting the Italian striker's ability but, there were also moments of controversy to go with it. That did not stop him becoming a cult favourite with supporters, during two-and-a-half seasons in which he scored 30 goals. And, of course, it was his assist that set up Sergio Aguero for the title-winning goal against QPR in 2012.

★ PABLO ZABALETA ▲

Manchester City's modern era is noted for featuring some of the world's most talented players but, in a popularity contest with fans, there is every chance the winner would be an uncompromising right-back from Argentina. Zabaleta's farewell ceremony at the Etihad in 2017 was one of the most emotional ever seen and he has been guaranteed a hero's welcome every time he has returned since.

★ SHAUN WRIGHT-PHILLIPS ▼

The flying forward's City career straddled the move from Maine Road to the Etihad but the England international is still a hero in the eyes of older fans who especially remember his incredible goal in the last minute of the 4-1 derby win over United in March 2004.

★ DAVID SILVA ▲

Ten seasons and ten trophies says it all about the Spanish magician. But let former City team-mate Gareth Barry tell you all you need to know about David Silva. "As an ex-pro now, you get asked who is the best player you played with," says the former England international. "There were so many but David Silva was incredible to play with. As a deep-lying player, getting your head up and looking for someone to pass to, he was magic at finding space. For his slight frame you just couldn't get the ball off him."

★ GLAUBER BERTI ◄

A left-field memory from the Etihad era, but the Brazilian became a cult hero with City fans after being an unused sub in 20 games in 2008/09. Finally, in the final home game, a 1-0 win over Bolton, he came off the bench with six minutes to go and his every touch was greeted with raucous cheers. It was his only ever City appearance.

★ PAUL DICKOV ▶

There are few players in City history more fondly remembered than Paul Dickov; certainly no player who only played in 10 games for the club at the Etihad. The striker, of course, wrote his way into the City record books for his work before the club moved to the new stadium but he returned from Blackburn for the 2006/07 season. Injuries limited him to just 18 games and two goals in that spell but "Dickie" is still a hugely popular figure in a media role at the Etihad these days.

★ NICKY WEAVER ▼

Like Paul Dickov, Weaver's part in City folklore was guaranteed before he moved to the Etihad. But he spent four seasons at the new home, largely as a back-up, and played at the stadium 15 times in his last season, 2006/07. But his most memorable Etihad role was the last game of the 2004/05 campaign against Middlesbrough, when he came on as an 86th-minute sub to allow David James to go and play up front!

★ SCOTT CARSON ▶

The veteran goalkeeper has spent four seasons with City, in part to add his experience to the younger keepers around him, and has rarely seen first-team action. But Pep Guardiola, always respectful of football history, brought him on with 20 minutes left in a 0-0 Champions League draw with Sporting Lisbon in March 2022. It meant the then 36-year-old was appearing in the competition 17 years after his last European game, for Liverpool.

★ OLEKSANDR ZINCHENKO ▼

The versatile full-back or midfielder was already popular with City fans well before the tragedy that engulfed his country, Ukraine, in 2022. But following the invasion by Russia, fans and team-mates showed their support for the Ukraine national team captain. And when Guardiola made him captain for the FA Cup trip to Peterborough in Zinchenko's next appearance, his legend grew that little bit more.

★ ALEKSANDAR KOLAROV ▼

The no-nonsense Serbian defender spent seven years at the Etihad and was part of the team that won the first trophy of the modern era, the 2011 FA Cup. He had an eye for a set-piece goal, scoring 21 times in 247 games and is fondly remembered as a key component of City becoming a team capable of challenging for the big trophies.

✴ NIGEL DE JONG ▶

The tough-tackling Dutchman played 137 games for City and no fan ever questioned his commitment in a single one of them. He only scored two goals in his time with the club but is rightly hailed for the first of them, a brilliant strike in a 2-1 win over West Ham in May 2011, which ended a run of nearly three full seasons without a goal.

✴ MICAH RICHARDS ▼

Injuries sadly limited this brilliant defender's career but you just have to see Richards' work as a TV pundit today to appreciate how much City means to him – and the feeling is mutual. "The highlight of my Man City career was being the first academy graduate to win the Premier League. Why? Because we produced something," he says. "The FA Cup was great. But to win the league with an Academy graduate, that's not something that happens that often. City hadn't done that, so to have played 30 games in a season when we finally became champions, that was special to me."

No.9 ★ TITLE TRIUMPH #3

After winning their previous two Premier League titles in such unforgettable fashion, Pep Guardiola's first Premier League crown in 2018 was very low key, in terms of late-season drama.

City fans were spared the nail-biting anxiety of a final day at the Etihad with everything to play for and, indeed, City were not even playing in the game which saw them crowned champions.

Instead, over the campaign, supporters were treated to one of the most dominant performances by an English champion side for many years.

The title coronation, when it came, arrived as early as April 15, a Sunday afternoon when City were not even playing, having won 3-1 at Tottenham the day before.

City's closest rivals Manchester United were in action on that Sunday when Jose Mourinho's side were upset 1-0 at Old Trafford by a West Brom team that was bottom of the table and under a caretaker manager, Darren Moore.

The Blues still had five games remaining and, a week later, the new champions were welcomed back to the Etihad in style by their adoring fans, and pulled off a thumping 5-0 win over Swansea.

Huddersfield were next up at home, and managed a plucky goalless draw, before City were officially crowned champions, three weeks after they had mathematically won it, with Vincent Kompany leading the by-now familiar celebrations as he lifted the Premier League trophy aloft.

Unlike the previous two occasions, this trophy presentation day brought with it a day without drama, and title celebrations began well before kick-off, among supporters at least.

There was also a great nod to City's proud history – and the title-winning team of 1968, exactly 50 years earlier – as members of that legendary Bell-Lee-Summerbee squad were welcomed onto the pitch.

A few days later, City rounded off their home season with a 3-1 win over Brighton as the Etihad said farewell to one of their favourites, Yaya Toure, playing his last game there.

It was the third time in seven years that City had won the league and the Etihad had been key to that success, with the stadium a fortress. Pep Guardiola's team won 16 of their 19 home league games, winning 14 straight home league matches from early September to late March.

But along with the silverware, came a host of records that reflected City's dominance.

A win on the last day at Southampton set a new record for most points with a magical 100 and the biggest winning margin, as they finished 19 points clear of second-placed United.

There were records for most away points (50), most wins (32), most goals (106) and biggest goal difference (+79) and most consecutive victories (18) ... the list went on.

"We cannot deny, we are so proud of the records," said Guardiola before the Saints game. "I am not saying we are the best [Premier League side ever] but we did the best season ever.

"Nobody scored more goals, more points. Now it's 97 so if someone wants to beat that record, they have to be good and win a lot of games. Today is a special day.

"To be considered one of the best, you have to win more. To be alongside United in the 1990s or Liverpool in the 1980s you have to win more.

"I am not saying we are a legend team, I am not saying we are better than them. No, because you have to make more years to do that, but in one season we were better than all of them in the history of the Premier League and the history of English football."

No.10 ★ THE BOSSES

★ KEVIN KEEGAN (2001-05) ▲
The former England star was in charge for the move to the Etihad and enjoyed many firsts – along with some mixed fortunes – in that opening season. He announced his retirement from football the following campaign and left in March 2005.

★ STUART PEARCE (2005-07) ▶
Formerly a player before eventually being appointed manager, Pearce almost led City to UEFA Cup qualification in his first few months but endured some tricky times in his next two seasons.

★ SVEN-GORAN ERIKSSON (2007-08) ◄

A quick stay in charge for the former England manager who led City to a top-ten finish, a place in the UEFA Cup and became the first manager since 1969/70 to win both derby games against United.

★ MARK HUGHES (2008-09) ▼

The ex-Wales boss spent 18 months in charge during a transitional period for the Blues but made an incredible mark in the transfer market, signing the likes of Vincent Kompany, Pablo Zabaleta, Kolo Toure, Carlos Tevez, Gareth Barry and Joleon Lescott – sowing the seeds for future glories.

★ ROBERTO MANCINI (2009-13) ▶

The dapper Italian was an instant hit with City fans, especially when he ended a 35-year wait for silverware by leading the club to victory over Stoke in the 2011 FA Cup final, at the end of his first full season in charge. He also, of course, masterminded the thrilling 2012 Premier League title win and for that reason alone – not to mention his legendary City scarf! – he is still an icon to City fans.

★ MANUEL PELLEGRINI (2013-16) ▼

The Chilean manager lifted City to new heights in Europe, taking the club to their first-ever Champions League semi, and led City to the 2014 Premier League and two EFL Cup final successes. In short, he continued the solid work laid down by Mancini and set supporters up for what was to come.

★ **PEP GUARDIOLA (2016-)** ▶

A record of 14 trophies and five league titles were the story of Guardiola's first seven years in charge at the Etihad. But let the man speak for himself when he describes his bond with the Etihad, the club and its supporters.

"I know the next chapter of this club will be amazing for the next decade. It happened over the last 10 years, and it will happen in the next 10 years because this club is so stable," said Pep when he signed a contract extension in the 2022/23 season.

"From day one I felt something special being here. I cannot be in a better place. I still have the feeling there is more we can achieve together and that is why I want to stay and continue fighting for trophies."

No.11 ∗ EURO NIGHTS

From Welsh minnows TNS all the way to European royalty like Real, Bayern and Barca, the Etihad has witnessed some truly unforgettable European nights over the past two decades.

Whether the UEFA Cup, the Europa League or, in more recent seasons, the Champions League; City have given supporters plenty of thrills, spills and, of course, the occasional heartache along the way.

By the time Real Madrid visited the Etihad for a thrilling Champions League semi-final in May 2023, which City won 4-0, the club had hosted 76 European games at the Etihad.

Along the way, Europe had also given supporters a new celebratory chant or, more accurately, dance that would take the football world by storm – 'The Poznan'.

As for the more serious on-field matters, those early tentative steps in the UEFA Cup had seen City progress to the point where, from 2017-23, the Etihad hosted a quarter or semi-final in the Champions League for six straight seasons.

That is a long way from a UEFA Cup qualifying tie in August 2003 when, after 25 years without involvement in a European competition, City played their first-ever competitive game at the Etihad – and beat Welsh side TNS 5-0.

"It was a huge game for them, and for us, because it was the first game ever at the Etihad," recalled one of the scorers that night, Robbie Fowler.

"We won 5-0 but it shows you the difference with Manchester City now and the quality of opposition City face every game in Europe. It was a quiet entrance into Europe, shall we say."

Quiet perhaps, but slowly City started making noise in Europe, reaching the UEFA Cup quarter-finals in 2009, beating Hamburg 2-1 at the Etihad, thanks to a winner from Felipe Caicedo, but failing to overturn a 3-1 first leg deficit.

A couple of years later came that legendary Poznan encounter, where an Emmanuel Adebayor hat-trick clinched a 3-1 win at the Etihad. And as City began to establish themselves as a Premier League force, the Champions League beckoned.

Napoli provided the first Champions League opposition at the ground, a 1-1 draw in September 2011, but the visit of German giants Bayern Munich three months later was a sign that City had truly arrived among the European elite, with goals from David Silva and Yaya Toure clinching a 2-0 win.

The following season brought Jose Mourinho's mighty Real Madrid to town, with a Sergio Aguero penalty earning a 1-1 draw in a group game many City fans remember equally fondly.

And while the Blues did not advance to the knock-out stage in their first two seasons, by 2013/14, they did and Barcelona visited in the Round of 16, picking up a 2-0 win with a goal from Lionel Messi.

That was just the start of City's rivalry with the Argentina legend because, a season later, the teams met in the Round of 16 once more. Despite two goals from Luis Suarez giving Barca a 2-1 win in the Etihad first leg, Joe Hart saved impressively from a Messi penalty with virtually the last kick of the game.

That season also included the highlight of Pep Guardiola bringing his Bayern Munich side to the Etihad for a group game in which Aguero scored a sensational hat-trick, including two in the final five minutes, to help City bounce back from 2-1 down to win.

The 2015/16 campaign saw City take an important step as Manuel Pellegrini led them to their first-ever Champions League semi and while the goalless draw with Real Madrid was hardly a classic, and required another superb showing from Hart, it was a sign that City had arrived.

It was the start of some incredible, high-stakes European nights.

The 2016/17 season saw City come back from an early Messi goal to hammer Barcelona 3-1, thanks to two from Ilkay Gundogan; before the Round of 16 brought an amazing, roller-coaster clash with Monaco and a 5-3 victory on the night (although an exit on the away goals rule).

The next two seasons brought English opponents to the Etihad in the quarter-finals, with City losing 2-1 to Liverpool, then beating Tottenham 4-3, in a second leg which the Blues won 4-3 but again lost on the away goals rule.

And, in the Covid-affected 2019/20 campaign, City had to wait over five months between the first and second legs of their last-16 tie with Real Madrid, eventually easing through 2-1 at a behind-closed-doors Etihad, with goals from Raheem Sterling and Gabriel Jesus.

A year later and City reached their first semi-final in five years, with Messi again the opposition, this time with French side PSG. A brilliant performance, and two goals from Riyad Mahrez, was more than enough to carry his team through to City's first European final in 51 years and their first ever in the Champions League.

No.12 ✶ TITLE TRIUMPH #4

There was more last-day drama as the 2018/19 title race came to a thrilling conclusion – although this time the Etihad was spared the nerve-jangling tension.

But what City supporters, and the Premier League in general, got instead was one of the most incredible title run-ins in the history of the English game between Pep Guardiola's men and Liverpool.

It ended with City crowned champions on 98 points, the second-highest ever points total in history, second only to the magical 100 they had amassed a year earlier.

It was no consolation for Jurgen Klopp's valiant runners-up that their total of 97 was the third best ever tally – that was an indication of just how close the race had been and how good the two teams were.

City would eventually win the title, on the final day yet again, with a thumping 4-1 win at Brighton. They had to recover from a goal down to do so – capping a magnificent run of 14 straight wins to clinch the title.

But it was the game before, the last home match of the season, that many supporters remember as one of their highlights as Leicester came to the Etihad and provided stubborn resistance.

By this stage, it was looking like City and Liverpool would win all their remaining games, which meant that a draw might prove to be as damaging as a defeat. So as the game reached the 70-minute mark, the Etihad was becoming anxious – until skipper Vincent Kompany took aim from 30 yards out and struck a brilliant winner – meaning the Blues maintained their one-point lead going into the final day.

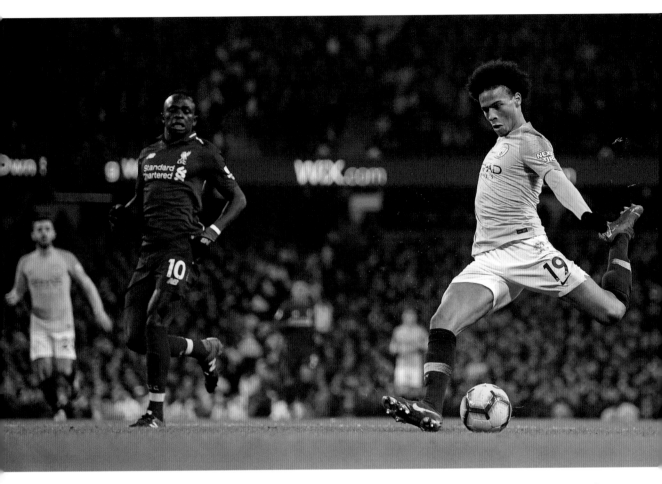

"One game left, and it will be so tough like today," Guardiola said afterwards. "We are away and we saw Brighton had a good game at Arsenal. But it is in our hands, don't forget we could have been 10 points behind if we lost to Liverpool here [in January]. We were seven points behind, but now we are in the last game and it is in our hands. It will be tough, but hopefully we will have the performance to be champions."

The Etihad had also been the scene of the other major turning point in the season, shortly after New Year's Day, when Liverpool visited.

The previous year had ended with Liverpool holding a seven-point lead at the top and, by the time they visited, Klopp's side were still seven points better off.

But on a thrilling Thursday night, Sergio Aguero and Roberto Firmino exchanged goals before Leroy Sane appeared on the end of a Raheem Sterling pass to clinch a 2-1 win.

It was Liverpool's only defeat of the season, while the only points that City would drop over the rest of the campaign would come in a 2-1 defeat at Newcastle at the end of January.

"I am proud of them, but not just today," Guardiola said after beating Liverpool. "We lost two games in four days, but you can't forget what they have done for 16 months. We knew that it was a final today, if we lose it is almost over.

"All credit to these incredible players. Both teams tried to search for each other, we were not scared, we had no fear, and we had a lot of pressure. I don't remember a league so tough, there are so many huge contenders fighting for the title. Every game is a final."

'All credit to these incredible players. I don't remember a league so tough'

No.13 ☆ STRANGE BUT BLUE

Here are some of the most unforgettable – or oddest – moments from a great 20 years.

☆ DAVID JAMES PLAYS UP FRONT
With City needing to beat Middlesbrough in the final game of the 2004/05 season to qualify for the UEFA Cup, Stuart Pearce sent England keeper David James up front for the last four minutes, plus injury time, and he won a penalty … only for Robbie Fowler to, sadly, miss the spot-kick.

It remains the only time in Premier League history an outfield player has worn the number one shirt. "In a bizarre way, it was a good experience but the first I knew was at half-time when 'Chappie' (kit man Les Chapman) said, 'I've got your shirt printed,'" recalls James.

"It was the first I knew about it! So late in the game, I looked over to the left-hand side and there's [substitute keeper] Nicky Weaver stood there and the board's going up, and I'm thinking, 'Why am I coming off?' And as I'm approaching the touchline, obviously Claudio Reyna goes off instead.

"So I think, 'Oh!' I get the shirt handed to me, put it on, and then run on the field and wonder, 'What am I supposed to do?'

"I think I won three or four headers, which I was really proud of. I kicked about eight or nine players. I think they were all Middlesbrough players. It was horrible! Put it this way, if I was manager I'd have been brought off after a minute."

☆ ADEBAYOR CELEBRATION
City striker Emmanuel Adebayor had been taunted by fans from his former club Arsenal throughout the game at the Etihad early in the 2009/10 season.

So when he connected with a Shaun Wright-Phillips cross to head City into a 3-1 lead, he had every right to enjoy his celebrations.

Unfortunately, Adebayor got slightly carried away and sprinted the length of the Etihad, to the OPPOSITE end of the field, to celebrate in front of the visiting Gunners supporters.

It was an incident correctly criticised by all parties but one that City fans still remember, more even than the 4-2 final scoreline.

☆ STEPHEN IRELAND'S SUPERMAN UNDERPANTS
One of the more surreal moments in Etihad history came when midfielder Stephen Ireland scored the winner against Sunderland in November 2007 and promptly dropped his shorts … to reveal the offending underwear.

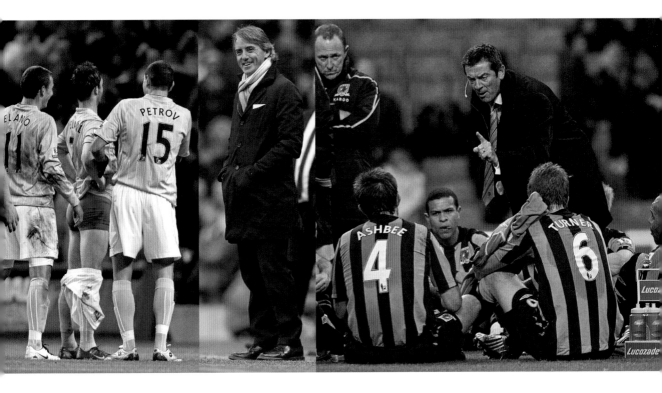

"It was funny, I didn't expect it to stick like it did," says Ireland. "It was changing room banter with the lads daring me to do something when I scored and I did and just went through with it.

"The fans put it in a song, which was amazing. I don't think you'd get away with it now with social media everywhere but I just got a warning letter."

★ MANCINI'S SCARF

Former City manager Roberto Mancini is obviously fondly remembered for leading the club into our trophy-winning era but there is another big reason he will always be an Etihad legend.

His scarf!

Being Italian, it was no surprise that Mancini quickly demonstrated a keen fashion sense when he arrived at the Etihad in 2009.

The former Inter boss marked his first game, against Stoke on Boxing Day, by sporting a traditional sky blue and white scarf while prowling the touchline.

In fact, he was still wearing it 45 minutes after the final whistle as he conducted media duties and, as City's success grew in the coming weeks, so did the popularity of the manager's fashion accessory.

The club soon manufactured replicas as a one-off before the end of the season and, the following campaign, demand meant they had to produce a whole lot more.

It was a reminder, in the era of superstar managers and players, that this one had a special bond.

★ ... AND IN THE OPPOSITION CORNER

City had been magnificent in racing into a 4-0 lead inside 36 minutes against Hull on Boxing Day 2008 and the opposition's manager had seen enough.

As dejected Hull players headed to the tunnel on the half-time whistle, their manager was heading back out ONTO the pitch, and gave his team-talk with players sitting around him in one of the penalty areas.

"I was walking off the pitch when I spotted Phil Brown heading onto it," Hull striker Dean Windass told the *Yorkshire Post* newspaper. "I just presumed he was going to make a point to the referee and thought nothing more of it. But then he shouted, 'Over here' and made sure we followed him."

The 3,000 visiting fans did see their team score in the second half, on the way to a final 5-1 scoreline, and they had certainly witnessed an unforgettable Premier League moment.

No.14 ★ CUP OF CHEER

As time ticked down on City's FA Cup quarter-final tie with Championship side Reading in March 2011, Micah Richards rose to meet David Silva's corner and powerfully headed in the only goal of a tense encounter.

It was enough to take City through to a derby semi-final with United, which also resulted in a memorable 1-0 win, before City ended a 35-year wait for silverware by beating Stoke in the final a month later, by – you guessed it – another 1-0 scoreline.

It was the start of over a decade of success for the club, with Richards' goal helping to book our date with destiny and drag us over the line after a gruelling Europa League clash with Dynamo Kyiv just three days earlier.

There have been many such classic cup moments, especially in the EFL Cup, which City have won six times in the years that we have called the Etihad home.

And there have been many memorable days and

nights. Who could forget the month of January 2019, for example, when the Blues played three home cup ties in 20 days and scored 21 goals in them?

A 7-0 FA Cup third round win over Championship side Rotherham was followed just three days later by a record 9-0 victory against Burton Albion in the first leg of the EFL Cup semi-final – still the biggest win at the Etihad.

As if 16 goals in two games, and three days, was not enough, before the end of the month, City hosted Premier League rivals Burnley and beat them 5-0 in the FA Cup, for good measure.

Oh, and there was also a league win crammed in there as well – 3-0 against Wolves – meaning City had actually scored 24 goals at the Etihad in 20 days, over four matches.

That month summed up City's domestic form that season as Pep

Guardiola's team became the first in football history to win all three English trophies in the same season, culminating in a League Cup final win over Chelsea on penalties and a 6-0 victory against Watford in the FA Cup final.

That was just the second FA Cup success of the Etihad era although City have enjoyed more glory in the EFL Cup, with some memorable home ties on the way to six final victories.

Alvaro Negredo bagged a hat-trick in a 6-0 win over West Ham in the home semi-final leg in 2014, Championship club Bristol City gave us a scare in the 2018 semi at the Etihad, which Guardiola's team only won 2-1 before clinching the tie away. City have also faced rivals Manchester United at home twice in EFL semis over the past two decades.

In 2020, City actually lost 1-0, but went through on aggregate, while, in 2010, the situation was reversed, with City beating United 2-1 but exiting the competition when we lost the return leg 3-1.

No.15 *
GOALS, GOALS, GOALS

The very first competitive game played at the Etihad Stadium – August 14, 2003 – may have been low key in some ways, but it was certainly a sign of things to come.

When Nicolas Anelka scored after 87 minutes of the UEFA Cup tie with Welsh minnows TNS, City had recorded a 5-0 win and rewarded the fans on hand with a taste of some of the goal frenzies that the stadium would witness in years to come.

It was the first of 64 occasions (as of 7-0 v Leipzig) that City scored five or more goals in a game at the Etihad.

Whether a 7-1 League Cup win over Barnsley a season later, or the 8-0 win over Watford in the Premier League in 2019, right up until 2022/23's Erling Haaland-inspired goal gluts; fans at the Etihad have not usually been short of goal action.

That was certainly true in January 2019, when Gabriel Jesus helped himself to four goals and City compiled a record (for the Etihad) 9-0 win over League One Burton Albion in the first leg semi-final of the EFL Cup.

Indeed, that month summed up what a goal magnet the Etihad has been for much of its two-decade existence.

In a little over a month, City won home games against Rotherham (7-0), Burton (9-0), Wolves (3-0), Burnley (5-0), Arsenal (3-1) and Chelsea (6-0). By the time that run ended, in a 1-0 league victory over West Ham, City had won six consecutive home games by a combined scoreline of 33-1.

Before the season was out, Pep Guardiola's team would provide fans with another memorable night, via a 7-0 win over German side FC Schalke in the last 16 of the Champions League.

That, incidentally, was one of an amazing total of 10 occasions that the Blues have scored seven, eight or nine at the Etihad.

The 'eight' might rank as many fans' favourite big-score game, as Bernardo Silva helped himself to a hat-trick and City beat Watford 8-0 in a Premier League clash in September 2019.

City were 5-0 up in the first 15 minutes on an incredible day that left Watford boss Quique Sanchez Flores to comment: "After 30 seconds we realised it would be tough, after 10 minutes really difficult and after 15 minutes it was impossible."

But in terms of overall significance, many will also point to the 6-0 win over Chelsea, as City were duelling with Liverpool for the title in February 2019.

Chelsea were a credible force, and would go on to finish the season in third place behind the two north-west rivals, but on one of those days that City, and Sergio Aguero, were virtually unplayable, Guardiola's men ran out handsome winners, with Kun missing a golden early chance ... and then going on to notch a hat-trick.

"If you have the ball as much as possible then the opponent does not have the ball," Guardiola said, summing up that day – but also City's overall philosophy. "Maybe one day they will change the rules but I think to score a goal you need the ball."

No.16 ⋆ LATE LATE SHOW

Okay, this conversation begins and ends with Sergio Aguero on THAT day in May 2012.

But that was far from the only last-gasp late show that City have treated Etihad fans to over the past 20 years.

In fact when Erling Haaland struck a last-minute penalty to beat Fulham 2-1 in November 2022, it was the 21st time City had scored a goal that won or drew a game for us in the 90th minute ... or later.

In fact, technically, it was the 22nd because, of course, City scored TWO goals after the 90 minutes were up to beat QPR and win the title in 2012.

But the very first game here, a 1-1 draw with Portsmouth in August 2003, featured a 90th-minute equaliser from David Sommeil and it has been a common theme ever since.

So, away from 93:20, here are a few other dramatic late goals for your consideration ...

⋆ Sergio Aguero v Villarreal, October 2011 ▶
Earlier in the title-winning season, the legend had warmed up for last-kick heroics when he turned in the winner at the far post with 93 minutes on the clock to make it 2-1.

⋆ Mario Balotelli v Spurs, January 2012 ▶
Every point would prove precious in this title race and the Italian turned one into three with a coolly-taken 95th-minute penalty that made it 3-2.

★ **Gareth Barry v Reading, December 2012** ▶
The midfielder headed in after 92 minutes as the reigning Premier League champions edged past the division's bottom-placed club 1-0.

★ **James Milner v Hull, February 2015** ◀
Utility man James Milner popped up two minutes into stoppage time with a free-kick that rescued a 1-1 Premier League draw. It came a month after the England star had scored a late winner in the 2-1 FA Cup success against Sheffield Wednesday.

★ **Kevin De Bruyne v Sevilla, October 2015** ▼
City were battling for a top-two finish in our Champions League group but were heading for a home draw until Kevin De Bruyne cut in, a minute into injury time, and made it 2-1.

★ **Kelechi Iheanacho v Swansea, December 2015**
The youngster did not know much about it but a shot by Yaya Toure after 92 minutes deflected off the striker's back and earned City a 2-1 win that took us back to the top of the table.

★ **Gabriel Jesus v Swansea, February 2017** ▼
A season later and the Welsh club were on the receiving end of another 2-1 defeat, this one in the 93rd minute when a Gabriel Jesus header was saved before the Brazilian tapped in the loose ball.

★ **Raheem Sterling v Southampton, November 2017** ▼
One of the latest of the late goals; 96 minutes had gone when Raheem Sterling curled in a magnificent winner that made it 2-1. Fans, players and the bench celebrated like we had won the league – which we did six months later.

And, of course, there has been plenty of drama just before the 90-minute mark. Who could forget these games that involved double late heroics?

★ v Sunderland, March 2012 ▲

City only had four league games left at the Etihad in the season and Manchester United looked to have the title wrapped up, especially with Sunderland leading 3-1 with five minutes left. But Balotelli, who had scored a first-half penalty, pulled one back with a superb shot and, just 69 seconds later, Aleksandar Kolarov snatched a vital equaliser.

★ v Bayern Munich, November 2014 ◄

The Germans had been reduced to 10 men after only 20 minutes but fought back from an early Aguero penalty to hold a 2-1 lead with just five minutes left. But, in shades of the QPR game two years earlier, Aguero pounced on two defensive mistakes, after 85 and 91 minutes, to give City a famous 3-2 win.

No.17 ★ TITLE TRIUMPH #5

There was to be no last-day drama when the Etihad saw Manchester City crowned champions of England for the seventh time in our history on May 23, 2021.

Instead, with just 10,000 fans watching on because of restrictions due to the Covid-19 pandemic, there was not only the chance to witness club skipper Fernandinho raising the Premier League trophy aloft.

There was also the opportunity to say goodbye to one of the true legends in City – and Premier League – history. With the Blues having won the title 12 days earlier without kicking a ball, those lucky City fans in attendance that day were spared the usual last-day nerves and came to pay tribute to Sergio Aguero, who had scored six goals in 20 appearances in his final season at the club.

But nobody had a sense for the occasion quite like Kun and in that final-day home game with Everton, and with City leading 3-0, he was thrown on as a 65th-minute sub and, of course, scored two goals almost immediately.

It was a fitting way for Aguero to say goodbye to the place he had called home for a decade and which had witnessed so many successes – including this, his fifth Premier League title.

City had entered the month of April with a commanding 14-point lead over closest rivals Manchester United, although the Reds had a game in hand.

And when City suffered a shock 2-1 home defeat to Leeds at the Etihad, just our second defeat in the last 35 league and cup games, that lead was suddenly down to 11.

But two solid away wins for City, at Aston Villa and Crystal Palace, meant that time was running out for Ole Gunnar Solskjaer's team, who slipped up in a goalless draw at Leeds in between those two big City victories.

It left Pep Guardiola's team needing just one more win to celebrate another title although, with City in the midst of reaching our first-ever Champions League final, that would have to wait a few more days.

The City boss made eight changes from the European semi-final win over PSG, and City were beaten 2-1 at the Etihad by Chelsea, who celebrated a last-minute winner from Marcos Alonso.

That was on Saturday May 8 but City did not have long to wait for the elusive win – although it was not one they were required to record themselves.

Leicester visited Old Trafford three nights later and came away with a 2-1 victory that meant City were crowned champions, for the third time in four years and the fifth in the last decade, without kicking a ball.

City won a thriller at Newcastle 4-3 and were pipped 3-2 at Brighton before returning home later in May for the final home game and that emotional farewell to one of the all-time greats.

It was a title success that manager Pep Guardiola dedicated to everyone at the club who had worked through the difficult Covid times.

"Here, the manager is the focus in the press conference and the players on the pitch, but there are a thousand people working behind the scenes to make this possible," he said.

"The Premier League is so nice and winning the Premier League is always the most important thing because every three days and every ten months we are fighting with the big teams and teams that might not fight for the Premier League but are so complicated to beat and we were there.

"In 10 years, Manchester City has won it five times. I think that everything this club has done in the last 10 years since Sheikh Mansour took over the club, Khaldoon as our Chairman, leading the rest of the people and we did it. A big compliment to everyone."

No.18 * HOME IMPROVEMENTS

Twenty years is a long time in football – and a long time in the life of a modern football stadium.
It is safe to say that, like all good homes, the Etihad has undergone some impressive improvements
over the years ... and welcomed some interesting visitors!

* HOME SWEET HOME ▲

The Etihad was winning awards for its ground-breaking design even before City moved in – accolades from bodies like the Royal Institute of British Architects and the Institution of Structural Engineers.

But since it became a full-time home for the Blues, it has become even bigger and better.

In August 2015, a 7,000-seat third tier was added to the South Stand, giving the ground its current 53,400 capacity.

And there are exciting plans in place for the near future, to develop the North Stand and take the Etihad up to a 60,000-plus stadium complex.

The proposals are for several connected all-weather facilities to be fully integrated into the stadium and centred around an expanded North Stand with one larger, single upper tier above the existing lower tier.

A covered City Square fan zone, with a capacity of 3,000 and a wide variety of food and drink outlets, new club shop, museum and hotel, are all proposed in order to offer a broad range of matchday and non-matchday activities.

★ STATUES ▼

Every home needs its decorations, and what could be better than adding some lovely touches to the exterior and paying homage to some of City's all-time greats in the process.

Statues of David Silva, Sergio Aguero and Vincent Kompany, all designed by world-renowned sculptor Andy Scott, were put up outside the stadium over 2021 and 2022 and serve as a daily reminder of the contributions made by those living legends.

"Sergio's contribution to Manchester City over the last 10 years cannot be overstated," Khaldoon Al Mubarak said when he announced the project.

"His legend will be indelibly etched into the memories of everyone who loves the club and maybe even in those who simply love football.

"It gives me great pleasure to announce that we will be commissioning an artist to create a statue of Sergio to live at the Etihad Stadium alongside the ones under construction for Vincent and David."

For former club skipper Kompany, there was even the chance to come back to the Etihad in a new role, as manager of Burnley in an FA Cup tie in March 2023, and he admitted going to "work" at a place where there was a statue of him outside was a surreal experience.

"It is hard to put into words how big an honour it is and I feel extremely grateful. That emotion is something shared not just by myself, but my family," said Kompany before that cup tie.

"My dad, when he saw it, it meant more to him than anyone. I think I got massive recognition from the club for who I was, not just as a player, as a competitor, maybe a leader in moments."

ETIHAD STADIUM

★ SEEING THE LIGHT ▲

A few concerned local residents may have initially taken to social media to say they thought they were being invaded by aliens – well, jokingly, anyway.

But City's light and laser shows before evening games have become a big part of the Etihad matchday experience.

After being trialled on a one-off basis, the shows proved such a hit that they became a regular feature of night games in the 2022/23 season, much to the enjoyment of fans ... once they got over their fears that Moonchester and his friends were launching an invasion!

★ FOOTBALL FRIENDS ◀▲

City have not been involved in every single football game ever played at the Etihad.

The stadium's reputation in world football has made it a popular choice for a number of other major matches – and from an England friendly with Japan in 2004 to a Conference Premier play-off final between AFC Wimbledon and Luton seven years later, the Etihad has hosted some great action.

Then there was the 2008 UEFA Cup final, in which Zenit St Petersburg beat Rangers, with tens of thousands of fans travelling down from Glasgow.

And in June 2005, the Etihad was the stage for England Women's opening game in the 2005 European Championships and a thrilling 3-2 victory over Finland, with Karen Carney grabbing a late winner.

★ SPORTS CITY ▶

As might be expected, given the proud multi-sports history of the whole area around the Etihad, our home has seen plenty of other sporting action.

During the Commonwealth Games in 2002, the Etihad – then the City of Manchester Stadium – was the host venue stadium, staging the ceremonies, plus all the athletics action and rugby sevens.

The athletics track, of course, has long since gone but the ground maintained its ties with both rugby codes.

Nearly 40,000 saw a rugby league international between Great Britain and Australia in October 2004, and the Rugby League's prestigious 'Magic Weekend' took place there for three seasons from 2012-14.

In October 2015, the rugby union World Cup also came to the Etihad, with England hammering Uruguay 60-3.

But maybe most fans' favourite non-football sports event came in May 2008 when a crowd of 56,337 saw City supporter Ricky Hatton beat Juan Lazcano – it was billed as 'Hatton's Homecoming' and, at the time, set a record attendance for a post-war boxing event in Britain.

★ SWEET MUSIC ◀

City fans provide this every time our team is at home, of course, but when it comes to the 'pros', the Etihad has hosted some of the greatest names in music history.

American rock band the Red Hot Chili Peppers were the first, but most certainly not the last, world-renowned act to grace the stage, in 2004.

From the Spice Girls, Take That and Taylor Swift to Beyonce and Jay-Z, the Etihad has catered to nearly all musical tastes in the last 20 years, with global mega-acts like U2, Coldplay and Bruce Springsteen selling out in minutes.

But perhaps the final note in Etihad music needs to come from the men themselves, the City-mad Gallagher brothers whose band Oasis set the attendance record for a concert at the stadium, 60,000 in 2005 – a gig captured in their live video of the occasion, *Lord Don't Slow Me Down*.

No.19 ⋆ TITLE TRIUMPH #6

With 15 minutes remaining in the 2021/22 Premier League season, Manchester City trailed Aston Villa 2-0 at the Etihad and were on the brink of surrendering the title.

A few miles down the M62, City's close rivals Liverpool were drawing 1-1 with Wolves, giving Jurgen Klopp's team hope that if they could snatch a winner at Anfield, they would be crowned champions, if City failed to beat Aston Villa...

There have been plenty of dramatic moments in Etihad history and, of course, nothing will ever top the first league title, won by Sergio Aguero and City in 2012.

But what unfolded in the final 15 minutes that May afternoon in 2022 is not far behind for sheer drama and importance.

Ilkay Gundogan, thrown on as a 68th-minute substitute just before Villa made it 2-0, gave City brief hope with a far-post header eight minutes later that set the stage for more heroics that would go down in Etihad folklore.

Two minutes after Gundogan's goal, Rodrigo drove an equaliser into the visitors' goal and the Etihad exploded.

There was more than a sense of inevitability, therefore, just three minutes later when Gundogan appeared at the far post once more to cap the comeback and secure a 3-2 win that guaranteed the title was coming back to the Etihad, regardless of Liverpool going on to win their game 3-1.

In all, there had been three goals in five minutes and little wonder that Pep Guardiola, a man and manager who has seen and done it all, was reduced to tears at the final whistle.

City had seen our character questioned in some sections of the media in the final weeks of the season but here, battling for the biggest stakes in English football, we had answered the critics.

"Always we believed. If you work for City or if you support City, you always believe. We never give up," said captain Fernandinho.

"It is an amazing feeling, a great feeling. After today's match, it was really emotional for us. I think it just showed the real Manchester City spirit. We fought until the end and we never gave up. In the end, the quality of our players made the difference and we are champions again."

That spirit had also been evident a week earlier when City scored twice in the second half to come from two goals down to draw 2-2 away at West Ham.

And five wins in the last six games hardly suggested a weakness in Guardiola's side. However, Liverpool's dogged consistency and a thrilling 2-2 draw between the two teams at the Etihad, in which Klopp's team twice came back from a goal down, set up the last day finale and all its attendant drama.

No.20 *
THE HITMEN
AND HAALAND

Erling Haaland's goalscoring exploits may have been amazing to behold after the Norwegian international made such an impact following his move to the Etihad in the summer of 2022.

But all he was doing, as he plundered three hat-tricks in his first four Premier League home games for the club, was continuing a proud tradition of City goalscorers over the past two decades.

From the first City hat-trick at the stadium – Nicolas Anelka's treble in a 4-1 win over Aston Villa in September 2003, barely a month after the club moved into the Etihad – all the way through to double delight in the Manchester derby in October 2022; there has been no shortage of natural-born goalscorers in club colours at our home.

That 6-3 derby win, the highest-scoring Manchester derby of all time, featured three apiece for Haaland and his team-mate Phil Foden, the first time two hat-tricks have been scored in the same game at the stadium.

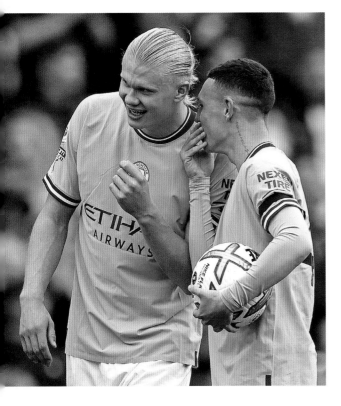

'I felt it today before the game and I felt it yesterday in the training.

'I felt a hungry club that wanted to attack this game, which is exactly what we did.

'It feels amazing, the atmosphere was insane. A hat-trick for me and Phil, it doesn't get better than that.'

Foden also became the 15th different player to score an Etihad hat-trick for City in the two decades that we have called it home.

Of course, all conversations about City goalscoring exploits always come back to club record goalscorer Sergio Aguero, the legend who scored nine of his record 12 Premier League hat-tricks at home.

He also set what looked like being a long-standing record when he hit back-to-back trebles on successive Sundays in February 2019; first in a 3-1 win over Arsenal, then in a thumping 6-0 victory against Chelsea.

Not to be outdone, Haaland did the same in the opening month of his City career, when he followed a hat-trick in the 4-2 win over Crystal Palace by adding another just four days later when he inspired a 6-0 win over Nottingham Forest.

Aguero is one of only two men to hit five in a game at the Etihad, in the 6-1 win over Newcastle in October 2015, an achievement matched by Haaland in the 7-0 win over Leipzig eight years later (the Norwegian also became only the third player, after Lionel Messi and Adriano, to hit five goals in a single Champions League game since the start of the 1992/93 season).

But Aguero also scored four on a couple of occasions. His old team-mate Gabriel Jesus, incidentally, can also claim the same record, hitting four in the 9-0 EFL Cup win against Burton and another quadruple against Watford in his final season with the club, 2021/22.

Another City favourite, Carlos Tevez, was also a star with an eye for the dramatic and smashed four league and cup hat-tricks in his time with the club.

But one thing is for certain about the art of big-haul goals at the Etihad: it is a trend that has become increasingly common with the passing of time.

In the first decade of football at the stadium, City players scored 10 hat-tricks on home turf. Between August 2013 and the end of January 2023, they poached another 27.

Incidentally, if you were wondering who the 15 City players are to score a hat-trick in a league or cup game at the Etihad, they are: Emmanuel Adebayor, Aguero, Anelka, Mario Balotelli, Bernardo Silva, Foden, Robbie Fowler, Haaland, Jesus, Riyad Mahrez, Alvaro Negredo, Robinho, Raheem Sterling, Carlos Tevez and Yaya Toure.

REGENERATING
OUR CITY

The Etihad stadium itself is only part of the story.
From derelict industrial land rose a magnificent complex
that has transformed the face of Manchester

It emerged from a great northern city's dreams of hosting the biggest sporting event on the planet.

And while Manchester never did land that Olympic Games we all wanted, the Etihad Campus and this corner of our great city have helped fuel the dreams and aspirations of so many Mancunians for two decades now.

As you have seen, it's been 20 eventful years since a sparkling new stadium, built amid the hopes that we would stage the 2000 Olympics, became our new home and in so doing sparked a football revolution.

And while it has been a roller-coaster of a football journey in many ways over those two decades, the development of the area surrounding the Etihad Stadium has been a non-stop success story of urban regeneration.

It is all a far cry from City's beloved Maine Road, the ground the club called home for 80 memorable years from 1923.

Packed into the terraced streets of Moss Side, the stadium was ahead of its time when it was built 100 years ago but ended up as an antiquated – if much loved – example of an 'old' football ground.

City moved with the times, and opened their Platt Lane training complex a few yards from Maine Road in the late 1970s, but it was a world away from the vision brought to east Manchester by the club's new owner Sheikh Mansour bin Zayed Al Nahyan when he took over in 2008.

The club had moved into the Etihad, and officially opened the ground as a football stadium in a glamour friendly against Barcelona in the summer of 2003, but Sheikh Mansour had a bigger, bolder vision than just hosting a successful European football club.

'While Manchester never did land that Olympic Games we all wanted, the Etihad Campus and this corner of our great city have helped fuel the dreams and aspirations of so many Mancunians'

The failed bid for the 2000 Olympics had not only resulted in the building of the Etihad Stadium but eventually saw the Commonwealth Games come to Manchester in 2002 – still one of the sporting highlights in this city's history – and left the local council looking for new tenants for their impressive new ground.

Along with the Etihad, then known as the City of Manchester Stadium, a sporting complex had been built to support those Commonwealth Games.

Those facilities – Sport City as it is still known today – had already helped renovate what had once been waste and derelict industrial land, including the old Bradford Colliery, in an area of the city known simply by locals as Eastlands.

And in December 2013, after nearly six years of planning and development, the club launched the City Football Academy (CFA), a state-of-the-art complex which fulfilled Sheik Mansour's vision of his club being at the heart of east Manchester's community, while also bringing through young football talent.

Built on derelict land, just a long goal-kick away from the Etihad Stadium itself, the new complex featured a 7,000-capacity mini-stadium – now, of course, the regular home of the successful City women's team – 16 outdoor pitches, six swimming pools and three gyms.

With the global City Football Group also based there, it provides a brilliant example of how modern football clubs are attempting to not only produce good young footballers, but good young people, while positively impacting the local community at large.

The CFA sits at the heart of the Etihad Campus and two-thirds of the football pitches there are dedicated to youth football.

Throw in education facilities, medical and sport science services, sleeping accommodation and parents' facilities, and it's clear why envious clubs from around the world come on fact-finding missions to this corner of Manchester.

And the CFA has proved such a success that the idea has been replicated across the globe by the City Football Group, with academies opened in Melbourne in 2015, New York three years later and then, in March 2021, the Montevideo City Football Academy, the very first of its kind in South America.

But, just as importantly for the Sheikh's vision for Manchester, the developments also included community outreach and urban regeneration programmes around the academy.

The Beswick Community Hub features the Connell Sixth Form College (named after Anna Connell, the founder of St Mark's Gorton, which later became Manchester City FC), a community leisure centre, the Manchester Institute of Health and Performance, award-winning public artwork and has even seen 6,000 trees planted.

There is also a stunning 60-metre pedestrian walkway that crosses Alan Turing Way and Ashton New Road and links the football stadium with the Campus.

And, of course, as was always the plan, the Etihad is about more than just the football. From Rugby World Cup games, to Ricky Hatton fights and numerous concerts, led by none other than City super-fans Oasis, the stadium and area have made their mark on the entertainment world at large.

Those dreams may have shifted from hosting an Olympic Games. But the CFA is still helping turn dreams into reality for thousands of young people, providing employment opportunities to the local community and truly placing itself at the heart of east Manchester.

There are also exciting development plans that will see the Etihad capacity rise to 61,000 and become the fourth-largest club ground in England, although all the new concepts are consistent with the long-held vision to establish the Etihad Campus and the wider area as a globally relevant and competitive sport, leisure and entertainment centre.

It explains why, since 2008, the City Football Group has overseen £700 million of investment into the Etihad Campus and east Manchester; investment which has supported thousands of jobs with the Group and its partners. This is all happening just a couple of miles from Hyde Road and the sight of City's first-ever permanent home ground in 1887.

But, while the Etihad Campus may be a world away from a Victorian era football ground, it has one thing in common with Hyde Road and Maine Road – it is OUR home; the place where dreams have been made for 20 years now, and hopefully will be for many decades to come.

CITY WOMEN
SETTING THE STANDARD

It's not just City's all-conquering men's team that have benefited from the superb facilities at the Etihad complex in recent years. Manchester City Women have also enjoyed an impressive run of success, with a whole new generation inspired to watch the team at the Academy Stadium.

The Blues won the Women's Super League in 2016, as well as finishing as runners-up on six occasions since 2015. They've also been prolific in cup competitions, lifting the FA Cup in 2017, 2019 and 2020, as well as the League Cup four times since 2014.

This silverware-laden era has come against a backdrop of booming attendances, with thousands regularly packing out the Academy Stadium to cheer on the Blues. And the City women have also graced the Etihad Stadium, with an incredible 44,259 people watching the Blues take on Manchester United in December 2022 – the historic local derby smashing the club's attendance record for a women's fixture by more than 13,000. With a winning football team and magnificent footballing facilities to match, the future certainly looks bright for the Blues...

From Manchester to Melbourne,
Montevideo and Mumbai...
we've come a long way from the days
of Maine Road and Platt Lane.
Our other home stadiums are spread
across multiple continents which now
gives City a global footprint

NEW YORK CITY

New York City Football Club is the first and only Major League Soccer team to play in the five boroughs of the Big Apple.

Since the club's 2015 inaugural season, New York City Football Club (NYCFC) has cemented its status as a cornerstone in the landscape of one of the world's most competitive and proudest sporting cities.

Winners of the 2021 MLS Cup – and bringing a major league championship sports trophy to New York city for the first time in over a decade – NYCFC was created for the city, offering a world-class soccer experience and a deep commitment to give back to New Yorkers through beautiful football, trailblazing spirit and football citizenship.

Majority owned by City Football Group, NYCFC plays the majority of home games at the iconic Yankee Stadium, which is also home to minority owner, the New York Yankees.

MELBOURNE CITY

Melbourne City Football Club is a professional side that competes in the major Australian domestic competitions, the A-League.

The club, formerly known as Melbourne Heart FC, was established in 2009, and was inspired by a vision for a broad-based community team, celebrating cultural diversity and sporting passion through football.

Becoming known as Melbourne City FC in 2014, the club is wholly owned by the City Football Group and plays its home games at AAMI Park, a 30,000-capacity stadium in the heart of Melbourne's sporting precinct.

Since its inception, the club has built a reputation as one of Australia's best on and off the pitch, with a proud history of youth development and on-field success for both men's and women's teams.

YOKOHAMA F MARINOS

City Football Group were announced as a minority shareholder of the Yokohama F. Marinos (YFM) in May 2014, providing access to CFG's training methods, medical care, sport science, team management and coaching know-how.

The partnership between Nissan Motors, the majority owners of YFM, and CFG marked the first significant foreign investment in a J-League club.

Yokohama F. Marinos were founded in 1972 as Nissan Motors FC before changing their name to Yokohama Marinos in 1993. In December 2019, the club were crowned J-League champions for the fourth time in their history, and the first time since 2004, finishing six points clear of rivals Tokyo FC.

Managed by Kevin Muscat, the club play at the Nissan Stadium in Yokohama.

MONTEVIDEO CITY TORQUE

City Football Group invested in Uruguayan football club Montevideo City Torque in April 2017. Initially founded in 2007 and known simply as Torque, the club was renamed Montevideo City Torque at the beginning of the 2020 season.

The team plays its home games at the legendary Estadio Centenario in Montevideo. Within the first three seasons under CFG ownership, the team achieved promotion to the Uruguayan Primera Division twice, the first time in its history in 2017 and back again in 2019. The team qualified for the Copa Sudamericana in 2021 and Copa Libertadores in 2022.

In March 2021, the club unveiled the Montevideo City Football Academy. The club's new home is the first of its kind in Uruguay, housing men's and women's teams, youth teams, club staff and community foundation projects.

GIRONA FC

In August 2017, City Football Group, together with Girona Football Group, acquired Spanish football outfit Girona FC in an equal partnership deal (44.3% by each party).

Girona have been promoted to the Primera División for the second time after having been close to this objective in the two previous play-offs. The club, founded in 1930, has experienced the best period in its history coinciding with the entry of City Football Group when promotion to Primera (2017) was achieved.

Girona FC's on and off-field potential, together with a positive academy track record, contributed to the rationale for the new investment by both stakeholders. The consolidation in the First Division, the construction of a Sports City, the renovation of the Montilivi stadium and the development of talent are the foundations for the future.

SICHUAN JIUNIU

In February 2019, City Football Group announced the acquisition of Sichuan Jiuniu in China League 2, together with CFG shareholders CMC, through China Sports Capital, and Manchester City partner UBTECH.

Based in Chengdu in Sichuan Province, Sichuan Jiuniu plays its home games at the 27,000 capacity Chengdu Longquanyi Football Stadium. As of March 2022, the club is now owned by CMC and CFG.

Sichuan Jiuniu was recently announced as one of the new partners of Therabody, along with Manchester City, Melbourne City and Mumbai City. Therabody is the creator of the world's first-ever percussive therapy device, which is used to accelerate recovery, reduce the risk of injuries and support optimal athletic performance. It is an example of how City can share information and best practice with their global clubs.

MUMBAI CITY FC

In November 2019, City Football Group agreed a deal to acquire a majority stake in Mumbai City FC, marking a major move into Indian football.

In 2021 Mumbai City FC were crowned Champions of the Hero Indian Super League after a 2-1 win over ATK Mohun Bagan at the Fatorda Stadium in Goa.

Mumbai City FC's victory saw them become the first team in ISL history to secure both the ISL Shield and the ISL Trophy, completing a double in the same season. In 2022, the club played its first game in the AFC Champions League, and in April became the first Indian football club to win a match in the competition.

The club plays its home games at the 8,000 capacity Mumbai Football Arena, which sits within the Andheri Sports Complex, a multi-purpose sports facility.

LOMMEL SK

In May 2020, City Football Group agreed a deal to acquire a majority stake in Lommel SK in the Belgian Second Division.

Lommel SK plays its home games at the 8,000 capacity Soevereinstadion, in the province of Limburg. Renowned for a strong Academy and focus on youth development, the history of the club dates back almost a century.

In July 2022, following consultation with the club's supporters, Lommel SK unveiled its new badge. The brand-new crest contains important and recognisable elements that characterise both the club's history and the city of Lommel. The new club logo acknowledges the past and embraces the future. Lommel SK also brought back its original 'stamnummer' '1986' to complete the circle.

ETSAC TROYES

In September 2020, City Football Group announced that Espérance Sportive Troyes Aube Champagne (ESTAC) had become its 10th club.

Founded in 1986, ESTAC calls the 20,400 capacity Stade de l'Aube home.

The club won the Intertoto Cup in 2001 and were Ligue 2 champions in 2014/15, finishing in fourth place, one point off promotion, when the 2019/20 season was suspended.

In September 2020, ESTAC integrated the City Football Group, representing a new chapter for the club. A few months later, the team were Ligue 2 champions for the second time and was promoted to Ligue 1. In the 2021/22 season, the team finished 15th, meaning they stayed in Ligue 1 for the first time in 16 years.

PALERMO

PALERMO FC

Founded in 1900, Sicilian club Palermo play in Serie B, the second tier of Italian football.

They have been winners of that division on five occasions, as well as winning the Coppa Italia Serie C in 1992/93. Palermo have also appeared in three Italian Cup finals (in 1973/74, 1978/79 and 2010/11). On the European stage, the club have made five appearances in continental competitions, all in the UEFA Cup and Europa League.

Palermo plays its home matches at Stadio Renzo Barbera, renamed in 2002 after the celebrated Palermo chairman of the 1970s. In 1984 the capacity was increased to 50,000 but for the 1990 FIFA World Cup, the stadium was renovated and the overall capacity reduced to 37,619.

In July 2022, it was announced that the club had been acquired by City Football Group.

BAHIA

Esporte Clube Bahia (EC Bahia) is a Brazilian Serie A club based in Salvador, Bahia State.

Founded in 1931, the Tricolor has won two national titles, 50 Bahia state championships and the championship of the northeast eight times. EC Bahia boasts a proud heritage, winning the first Brazilian Championship in 1959 and being the only club outside of the south of Brazil to win two league titles. EC Bahia also has a successful women's team, who compete in the top flight of the Brazilian championship and are six-time Bahia State champions.

In line with a current trend in the Brazilian football market, in April 2023 EC Bahia created a new entity, Esporte Clube Bahia SAF (Bahia SAF), to replace it as a football team and carry on its impressive heritage.

In May 2023, City Football Group became the majority shareholder of Bahia SAF, holding 90% of its shares.

CLUB BOLIVAR

Club Bolivar joined the City Football Group family as its first Partner Club in January 2021.

Founded in 1925 and based in La Paz, Club Bolívar is the most successful team in Bolivia, with 30 national titles, one qualification for the Copa Sudamericana final and two-time Copa Libertadores' semi-finalists.

As a CFG Partner Club, Club Bolivar is able to access a wide breadth of expertise, proprietary technology, best practice, and strategic advice developed by City Football Group through its multi-club structure.

The club has two stadiums. Estadio Libertador Simón Bolívar is only used for training sessions and friendly matches.

Estadio Hernando Siles, which holds a capacity for 41,143, is the club's main stadium, and is used for official matches.

MAINE ROAD
AND ETIHAD
MISCELLANY

Recalling some final weird and wonderful memories from both of our stadiums

MAINE ROAD INVINCIBLES

Surprisingly, City have only once gone an entire league season at Maine Road without defeat when the club went up as Second Division champions in the 1965/66 campaign. For 17 months the Blues were undefeated at home in the league. The Blues have clocked up 100 goals or more in the league on five occasions. The record is 108 set in 1926/27 when finishing third in Division Two and the figure was equalled for the 2001/02 season, with Stuart Pearce missing a last-minute penalty in the final game and blowing the chance of setting a new record and completing his own personal century of goals scored in his career.

THE ORIGINAL GOLDEN GOAL

Long before certain cup competitions were settled by the Golden Goal rule (or 'next goal wins!' as every schoolkid used to shout as the playtime bell rang), City used to have their own version of the Golden Goal. A stamped four-figure number would be inside the matchday programme and when the first goal was scored, the number of seconds was calculated and that was the Golden Goal. It was easy to identify the winner after a 0–0 draw because there was always one time printed as '0000'. The winner won something like £100.

ITALIAN JOB IS SHORT AND SWEET

City played in The Anglo-Italian Cup on only one occasion in September 1970. The winners of the League Cup met the winners of the Italian Cup on a two-legged basis. City played Bologna away in the first leg, losing 1–0 in front of a 28,000 crowd. The return leg ended in a 2–2 draw at Maine Road in front of a respectable 25,843 fans and that was the sum total of the Blues' involvement. Fans were, however, less impressed with another dual nation competition – the Anglo-Scottish Cup. Formerly known as the Texaco Cup, it consisted of three group games with the winners meeting Scottish opposition. Only 11,167 turned up for City's only home game in the competition – a 3-1 win over Sheffield United on August 9, 1975.

EVERY DOG HAS HIS GAME DAY

On the day after Guy Fawkes Night 1920, the Main Stand at City's Hyde Road ground burned to the ground and with it all the club's records. Worse still, City's faithful hound 'Nell' also perished in the flames. The cause was not, as first suspected, a firework but a stray cigarette butt. Several Moss Side strays have enjoyed a moment of fame by doing a lap of the Maine Road pitch and evading stewards with a feign and burst of pace that would inevitably have the Kippax roaring for the current manager to 'sign him up!' One cheeky mutt even ran up to the goalposts at the Platt Lane end and promptly cocked his leg up. Barefaced cheek!

MANCHESTER RAIN FAVOURS THE REDS

Maine Road only played host to one abandoned Manchester derby. The game was a league match played on August 27, 1960. It was abandoned due to a waterlogged pitch with the score at 2-2. City's scorers were Denis Law and Joe Hayes; United's were Dennis Viollet and Alex Dawson. A crowd of 51,927 were in the ground and had to head to the exits early. The bad news is that when the match was replayed, it ended in a 3-1 win for United on March 4, 1961, watched by 50,479 fans.

MAINE ROAD STILL INSPIRES NOEL

Maine Road provided the inspiration for a new Noel Gallagher single cover *Council Skies*, and it came about by chance, explains Noel: "The song itself is about finding young love on a council estate, the hopes and dreams you have underneath, spending each day dreaming underneath the council skies. It just set off a load of images in my head and that is why we ended up doing the cover shot on the old Maine Road centre circle." The cover shot idea originally started life as something completely different and Noel wasn't even aware that anything still remained connected with Maine Road having never visited our former home of 80 years since the club's departure. "I just happened to say to my driver to go to where Maine Road used to be and we found it, though it was difficult because you can't get your bearings around there anymore. There was someone there saying, 'You know that is the centre circle?' I was like 'no way' and I thought, 'Oh wow, this is the shot!'"

MANAGERIAL MERRY-GO-ROUND

The shortest period of time a manager was in charge at Maine Road was Steve Coppell's month-long reign in 1996. There was a high number of managerial appointments stemming from the time John Bond quit in 1983. Twelve bosses in 18 years equated to an average of 18 months for each boss. The overall average is three years and six months. Prior to 1983, it was an average of almost five years in the manager's chair. Thankfully, our current manager is happily enjoying an extended period in the City hotseat, and long may it continue.

LAP OF THE PITCH TRADITION

It was once tradition for a tracksuited youngster to run out before the Blues came on at Maine Road and run around the perimeter of the pitch. There have always been kids that walk on the pitch with the City players and have a kick-around with one of the players but, as for official club mascots, 'Moonchester' was the first real mascot City had. The blue alien is popular with the Junior Blues and in December 2001 the club introduced 'Moonbeam', Moonchester's female companion.

TV EVANGELIST BILLY'S MAINE ROAD GIG

In May 1961, after the football season had ended, the Blues' Maine Road ground became home to American TV evangelist Billy Graham, who preached to crowds of up to 35,000 a time during his stay in the city. Graham was a counsellor to American presidents and travelled the globe to become perhaps the best known Christian evangelist in history – with a number of appearances in the UK. Seats were temporarily installed on the Kippax terracing and the proceedings were broadcast live to another venue in Coventry. At this time there were no gates in the Kippax's perimeter wall leading to the pitch and so special scaffolding steps were erected to allow attendees to climb over the wall and on to the pitch for blessings.

SINGING THE BLUES

City supporters have sung many songs over the years but it wasn't until 1990 that *Blue Moon* became the fans' anthem. The 1970s were a great time for new songs and the Kippax favourites included the following: from the tune of *Lily the Pink* came *Colin the King* for Colin Bell; *Sha-la-la-la-Summerbee* – self-explanatory; Dennis Tueart's song was *Dennis Tueart King of all Geordies*; and *Rodney, Rodney* for Rodney Marsh, who later admitted it gave him goosebumps every time he heard it. There are more common and, in many cases, unprintable football songs heard at Maine Road but the ever-inventive Blues' fans were always coming up with originals like a customised version of the Oasis classic *Wonderwall*, and *I'm Dreaming of a Blue Wembley*.

AUTO FANS VOTE WITH THEIR FEET

City's record in the Auto Windscreen Shield competition is easy enough – played one, lost one. Arguably one of the lowest points in the club's history, City played Mansfield Town at Maine Road on December 8, 1998, and lost 2–1 in the first round (north) section with Danny Allsopp scoring our goal. The game itself was unimportant and the trophy meant nothing to City fans; most of them saw it as little more than a stark reminder as to how far the team had slipped since the glory days. It's more uplifting to think that just over 25 years since that game, City were celebrating a historic Treble. How football fortunes can change...

FRANNY THE SPOT-KICK KING

Franny Lee was the club's most successful penalty-taker ever during the Maine Road era with 46 penalty kicks successfully dispatched in his time at City. Lee famously won many of the penalties himself. Dennis Tueart scored an impressive 24 times from the spot, including several double strikes. Ken Barnes, father of City legend Peter, scored a hat-trick of penalties against Everton in December 1957 in a 6–2 win at Maine Road. Kevin Bond scored penalties in the 44th and 45th minutes of a home game against Huddersfield Town in April 1984 to bring the scores level at 2–2, but the Blues still lost 3–2.

MAINE ROAD WATERING HOLES

Everyone will recall their own favourite watering holes for a pre or post-match pint during the Maine Road days. The Gardeners Arms and The Osborne on Summer Place, to the rear of the Kippax, were two of the most popular, while The Claremont, The Welcome, The Beehive and The Friendship could also be found full of home fans on matchdays. The Parkside was another favourite and was the closest pub to the ground.

WHEN THINGS GOT TASTY

Referee Peter Willis once had a pie thrown at him after sending off a City player at Maine Road. He later commented that he didn't mind because the pie was quite tasty! Of the red cards shown to City players, some have been more memorable than others. In September 1962, Bert Trautmann was sent off for expressing dissent against West Ham at Maine Road. His dismissal saw the Blues collapse and lose 6–1. Ray Ranson and Tommy Booth were both sent off during a 'friendly' with Real Madrid in December 1979 and Mike Doyle once received his marching orders for punching Leighton James.

CAN I MIND YOUR CAR, MISTER?

One of the time-honoured traditions of a Maine Road matchday was being asked this question by youngsters looking to make a bit of pocket money. "My dad used to work for Coca-Cola, and when you parked up anywhere on one of the side streets it always happened," recalls Gary James. "He had a van from Coca-Cola, with logos all on the side. We got out of the van and inevitably loads of kids were waiting, 'Can I mind your car, mister?'. So my dad actually said, 'If you're here when I come back, you can have some Coke'. Usually there was no-one there when we returned but one time, this lad — he was only about four or five — he just stood there, 'I minded your car, mister.' So my dad got a bottle of Coke out and gave it to him."

TESTIMONIAL TRIBUTES

The last testimonial at Maine Road was thoroughly deserved and a crowd of over 25,000 turned out to pay tribute to Paul Lake, whose battle against injury stretched over five long years. Goalkeeping legend Joe Corrigan had a benefit match on November 7, 1979 as City beat Werder Bremen 4–0 at Maine Road. Paul Power, Mike Doyle and Colin Bell have all had testimonial games during the 1970s and 1980s.

WHEN THE CHIPS ARE DOWN...

In an incident fondly remembered to this day as 'Chipgate', the Etihad crowd received news that was difficult to stomach when we played Newcastle in November 2011. As the half-time whistle blew and the players headed back to the dressing room with a two-goal lead, an announcement informed our fans: "We are very sorry, chips are unavailable on the concourse today." Cue chants of: "Who ate all the chips?!" An issue with the gas supply meant they were unable to be heated up. However, the club made amends with a two-for-one food offer for the next home game against Norwich – and City fans were treated to a feast of goals as we demolished the Canaries with a 5-1 win.

WE LOVE YOU, ALAN, WE DO

Our Europa League fixture against Red Bull Salzburg in 2010 may be difficult to recall for some, but it was a night that Alan Douglas Borges de Carvalho will never forget. City were two goals ahead when the Brazilian came off the bench and was introduced simply as 'Alan' – to the amusement of a crowd that was accustomed to the outlandish nicknames of his compatriots. From then on, chants of "Alan, Alan, give us a wave!", "We love you, Alan, we do" and "Alan is Superman!" were belted out from the stands. "I'd just like to thank the City fans for the reception they gave me," said the Salzburg man afterwards. "I appreciate the affection and all the support you've all shown me. I love you guys!"

SIMPLY THE BEST

City fans have loved their new ground since it opened two decades ago, and in 2019, a study confirmed what we always knew – that the Etihad is the best stadium in the world. The study took in criteria such as season-ticket prices, smart technology, accessibility, eco-credentials, transport links, seating capacity ... and even the cost of a pint! The study examined clubs who had won their respective domestic leagues across Europe and further afield, making City the crème de la crème of all the continents...

UNLEASH HELL!

The Etihad takes inspiration from the Romans, with its pitch located six metres below ground level. This is a design feature commonly found in ancient amphitheatres and gladiatorial arenas, and creates an atmospheric setting, with the stands towering over the grass below. It's intended to feel intimate for the City players on their home turf, while perhaps intimidating for the visiting contingent. It also ensures that City fans across the stadium have an excellent view of the action, with brilliant sight-lines to the pitch, wherever they are sitting.

BEANIE THE HORSE

After a run of 13 defeats in 16 matches, manager Stuart Pearce and his struggling City side were in need of some urgent salvation. In September 2006, for a crucial Premier League game against West Ham, up stepped a new recruit to help us gain three much-needed points – a toy horse. "My wife Liz and my daughter Chelsea had decided they would come up to the game and Chelsea said to me that Beanie the horse should stand next to me on the touchline," Pearce revealed. "Beanie was her idea of a lucky charm for me." Beanie's appearance did the trick as two Georgios Samaras goals delivered a vital victory at the Etihad.

DRAWING BLANKS

The 2006/07 campaign was one of extremes on the home front. Unbeaten in our first eight games at the Etihad, a Samaras brace helped us beat Everton 2-1 on New Year's Day before we embarked on the worst scoring run on home turf in our history. Blackburn started the rot, winning 3-0 at the Etihad, and we had still to find the back of the net when neighbours Manchester United arrived for the final home game of the campaign in May. A 79th-minute penalty gave us the opportunity to cancel out Cristiano Ronaldo's opener and end our long wait for a goal, but the pressure was too great for Darius Vassell, who saw his spot-kick easily saved.

RECORD HOME RUN

Following a difficult end to the previous season, City bounced back by setting a new top-flight club record of nine straight home league wins at the start of the 2007/08 campaign. A 1-0 victory against Manchester United was the highlight of a run that also saw us beat Derby County, Aston Villa, Newcastle United, Middlesbrough, Birmingham City, Sunderland, Reading and Bolton Wanderers in front of our supporters. City's winning streak came to an end during the festive period, as Blackburn Rovers held us to a 2-2 draw at the Etihad, and our unbeaten record was eventually broken by Arsenal in a 3-1 defeat in February.

HARD DUNNE BY

A superb captain who won City's Player of the Year award a record four times, Richard Dunne also holds the unwanted title as the scorer of the most own goals in our history. He found the back of his own net six times while playing for City, the first of which came at the Etihad during a game against West Bromwich Albion in December 2004. We had led through a Nicolas Anelka free-kick until Dunne chased a long ball back towards his own goal and allowed it to strike him on the shin, which sent the ball past the onrushing David James from 20 yards out. It should be said the own goals often occurred because he was the last man, making the last-ditch effort to prevent us conceding!

'I wouldn't mind appreciating one more big game at Maine Road, but where we are now ... these are the glory days'

Noel Gallagher

'I have loved playing here with all of you behind us, and I know the players have, too'

Pep Guardiola